LIVING FOR CHRIST IN A CARNAL CULTURE

DEBORAH SPINK

Called: Living for Christ in a Carnal Culture

www.RegularBaptistPress.org • 1-800-727-4440
Printed in U.S.A.
RBP5531 • ISBN 978-1-64213-760-6

Contents

Preface

The church in Corinth was looking for answers. As new Christians in a morally corrupt environment, they needed to know how to live. Apparently, Paul had written to them earlier (1 Corinthians 5:9), giving instructions for godly living, and they replied but had questions (7:1).

So in 1 Corinthians Paul answered their questions. He also wrote about issues the church was struggling with, including division, carnality, and immorality. And he addressed questions regarding marriage, divorce, and the Lord's Supper. Consequently, this letter is a wealth of practical information for the church today.

During the apostle's second missionary journey, he went to Corinth. Acts 18:1–8 describes his time there: Aquila and Priscilla had recently arrived from Rome, since Claudius had commanded all Jews to leave. Though Aquila and Priscilla had been uprooted from their home, they demonstrated hospitality to Paul, allowing him to share their new home and business in Corinth.

With his practical needs taken care of, Paul was able to teach and preach, and "many of the Corinthians believed." Paul remained in Corinth about eighteen months. He wrote 1 Corinthians about three years later.

Corinth was a wealthy port city, famous for its temple to Aphrodite, "the goddess of love," with its one thousand prostitutes. The Greek word *korinthiazomai,* which is interpreted "to act the Corinthian," came to mean "to practice fornication" or "to be immoral." The city was known for everything sinful.

As in the days of Corinth, we live in an ungodly world where truth is blurred. Today we struggle with much of what the church at Corinth struggled with. Paul's letter to the Corinthians gives us insight into how to answer the issues that plague the church today, encouraging us to live for Christ in a carnal world. As you study, approach each lesson with an open mind, praying that God will make clear to you His answers for today's questions.

LESSON 1

Unity in the Church

1 Corinthians 1:1–17; 3:1–9

THERE IS NOTHING MORE disheartening than division in the church. Dividing over theological issues is one thing, but that is rarely the case in local churches. More likely, division in a local church stems from power issues, personality clashes, or pride. Paul begins his letter to the Corinthians by addressing the important issue of Christians maintaining unity as they labor together for Christ's glory.

Sanctified

Read 1 Corinthians 1:1–9. Paul begins the book with a greeting and an introduction before addressing the first issue.

1. Paul was traveling with Sosthenes, who was also sending greetings to the church. According to Acts 18:12–17, who might Sosthenes have been?

2. In 1 Corinthians 1:2 how does Paul describe the believers in the church at Corinth?

3. Who besides the Corinthians are "called to be saints"?

4. (a) Write a dictionary definition of *saint.*

   (b) According to Ephesians 1:4, what are believers chosen to be?

   (c) How does that fit with the definition of a saint?

5. According to Romans 8:29, what are believers predestined ("predetermined") to be?

God's plan is that believers become more and more like Him. His choosing in Ephesians 1:4 and predestination in Romans 8:29 have everything to do with being conformed to His image. That is what He has chosen for us! He will conform us and sanctify us ("set us apart," "make us holy") until we are glorified if we allow His Spirit to work in us. Paul reminds the Corinthian believers of this truth: we are saints—now act like it!

There are three stages of sanctification, or "saintification." The first is positional sanctification, which occurs at salvation. Therefore, this stage is in the past. God sees us as holy the moment we accept Christ's blood offering to cover our sins. The second stage is progressive sanctification, which is in the present. From the moment we are saved, we are to be growing to look more and more like the image of God. The final stage is future, which is perfect sanctification. This will take place when we see Jesus and no longer have to worry about sin.

6. Read 1 John 3:1–3. What statements describe these stages of sanctification?
   • Positional

- Progressive

- Perfect

Guaranteed

Next, in 1 Corinthians 1:4–8, Paul gives thanks for these believers, even though his letter addresses numerous problems in this church. Paul views the Body of Christ in Corinth with grace. He knows the Corinthians aren't perfect, but he is still thankful for them and Christ's work in them. Can we view our church family that way—being thankful for the work Christ is doing in each one's life instead of focusing on how far each needs to go? Paul recognized the grace of God in his own life and extended it to others.

7. Read 1 Corinthians 1:5–7.
   (a) What did Paul recognize in the Corinthian believers?

   (b) What phrases show the origin of spiritual gifts (vv. 4–5)?

We cannot take credit when God chooses to use us—our gifts come from Him. Believers in the church at Corinth were gifted in knowledge and utterance, or reasoning and communication. They knew the Scriptures and were skillful defenders of them.

8. What guarantee in verses 8–9 is true for believers today as it was for those in the church at Corinth?

The Corinthian believers were "confirmed" unto the end, that is, guaranteed. Though Paul was going to confront the church in this letter, he reminded them that as believers in

Christ they were guaranteed until the end because "God is faithful" (v. 9).

9. What other verses do you know that show believers are guaranteed ("given security to") until Christ comes again?

Read 1 Corinthians 1:10–17 and 3:1–9.

10. After his greeting, Paul addressed the first issue in the church. What was it?

11. What two things does verse 10 encourage the Corinthian believers to do?

12. Read Philippians 2:1–8, where Paul also speaks of unity. How can a group of people with a variety of opinions be unified, according to verses 3–7?

Can you imagine how these attitudes would change the church community? There would be no self-promotion or prideful opinions, but a constant looking to the good of each other and the church. With each one serving the needs of the other, there would be no division.

Used by God

13. According to 1 Corinthians 1:11–13 and 3:4, what was dividing the congregation in Corinth?

In those days, baptism identified a person as a follower of the one who did the baptizing or of the one the person was baptized for. Consequently, the members of the church in Corinth were partial to whoever had baptized them or whoever had been influential in their salvation and growth.

14. According to 1 Corinthians 3:5–6, how do servants of God work together to bring someone to Christ?

15. Read 1 Corinthians 3:4–7.
    (a) Describe how a variety of people could be involved in bringing someone to Christ.

    (b) How did you come to Christ?

    (c) How is salvation ultimately attained?

16. How does 1 Corinthians 1:17 affirm that salvation is apart from baptism?

17. Many servants of God may have a part in our salvation and growth. They are "laborers together." What two words (metaphors) describe us in 1 Corinthians 3:9?

The field and the building belong to God. Those who plant or build are simply tools used by God, and each is simply one worker among many. We are to be followers of God, not people. While we plant, water, or reap, we need to remember we are only a hoe, a hose, or a sickle in the Master's hand—to seek His glory, not our own.

18. In 1 Corinthians 3:1–3, what words does Paul use to describe someone who is causing strife or division by elevating human leadership?

A carnal Christian is controlled by fleshly desires rather than by the Holy Spirit. When we are following our flesh, division will result. Strife, dissension, and division are all marks of immature Christians.

19. Read the verses below and identify the way we are to respond to those who cause division.
    - Romans 16:17

    - 2 Thessalonians 3:6, 14

Sometimes churches with many staff members can become divided as people choose their favorite pastor. Even churches with several spiritual leaders or teachers can split because of allowing a person to take the place of God in their loyalties.

The problem can also come from power hungry leaders who, because of jealousy, promote themselves rather than the Savior. In trying to gain control, they divide the church.

Unity is, therefore, a sign of spiritual maturity and godliness. Paul speaks of the Corinthians as "babes," who are not ready for meat because of their envying, strife, and divisions. In a dog-eat-dog world, the church should be a place of unity and humility.

Read John 17:20–22. Christ's plan for the church is that Christians be one. It's time to put the unity of the Body over our own selfish conceits or desires.

Application

How can you apply what we have studied?

First, support your church leaders. Do you remember you are following Christ, not a man? Do you have a favorite, and if you do, do you show favoritism? How can you support each church leader in that person's role?

Second, be an integral part of the team. Every part of the body is important and is needed. How do you actively seek the good of the church and the glory of God as you "do nothing through strife or vainglory"? As you serve on a committee, be aware whether you are seeking the best for the church or are forcing your opinion. What do you do to bless the rest of the "choir"? How can you focus on encouragement to others rather than criticism?

Third, actively seek to plant, water, hoe, and reap! Share the gospel as the Holy Spirit gives you opportunity. Recognize that you are only a part of the process; do not get discouraged if the Word seems to fall on fallow ground. Your job is to spread the seed; it is God Who gives the increase. That tract you leave may be just the right words, or amount of water, for the seed already planted to sprout! What are you doing to prepare for opportunities to share the gospel?

As a mature, Spirit-filled Christian, you will be looking to sow unity, humility, and servanthood in your church. There is no better way to support your church leaders and bring joy to your pastor!

LESSON 2

Our Weakness, God's Power

1 Corinthians 1:18—2:16

THE CHURCH CAN FALL into the trap of holding in higher esteem those who are successes in the world than those who are not. For example, wouldn't the well-educated CEO be a better Sunday School teacher than the simple farmer? Can God really use an uneducated and unknown person to serve Him?

The church at Corinth was divided. One of the causes was a misunderstanding of a person's ability as opposed to God's power. The church was splitting based on allegiance to individuals instead of to God, Who enables His servants. He should have received all the glory.

The Greeks highly valued worldly wisdom and philosophy, which they thought told them the meaning of life, their purpose, and their destiny. To make matters worse, countless philosophers had their own philosophies and followers. There were, therefore, many factions. This cultural characteristic carried over into the church, it seems. Apparently, some in the Corinthian church were still clinging to the philosophical beliefs they had embraced before salvation. So they continued to prize human wisdom even as they trusted in Christ.

The "Wise" but Foolish

In recent years, the adoration of human wisdom and philosophy has been on the rise. Many of the younger generation idolize academia, debate, and philosophy. We see this growing in Christian circles as well as secular. Young people are leaving the faith, questioning absolutes, and embracing relativism and humanism. So 1 Corinthians 1:18–31 speaks to us today just as much as it did to believers in Paul's day.

1. Read 1 Corinthians 1:18–31.
   (a) According to verse 18, what is foolish to the unsaved?

   (b) How do you see that same view in our world today?

2. In verse 20, Paul alludes to Isaiah 29:14. Read the following verses and identify whom they refer to when they talk about the wise, the scribe, and the disputer of this world? (Tip: Pay close attention to the first verse in each passage.)
   • Isaiah 29:10–14

   • Matthew 15:1–9

Mere human wisdom is bound to fail. The Jewish leaders of Paul's day could not accept that the One Who had died on the cross could be God's Chosen One. Their wisdom had them looking for a political king, not a personal Savior. Even as the Greeks prized wisdom and Paul argued that wisdom does not bring anyone to God, he said that the preaching of the cross does (1 Corinthians 1:18). Human wisdom apart from divine revelation is pure foolishness. Romans 1:22 refers to the unsaved when it says, "Professing themselves to be wise, they became fools."

3. Read 1 Corinthians 1:21–25.
   (a) How was "Christ crucified" a stumbling block to the Jews (v. 23)? (See Matthew 12:38–40; Romans 9:31–33; 1 Peter 2:6–8.)

   (b) How was it foolishness to the Greeks?

   (c) Do you see similar attitudes in the world today? Explain.

4. (a) Upon a person's faith in Jesus Christ, what does Christ become to that person (1 Corinthians 1:24)?

   (b) How has Christ become God's wisdom and power to you?

5. According to 1 Corinthians 1:26–28, who has God "chosen" and "not chosen"?
   - Chosen

   - Not chosen

A lady of noble birth once remarked that she was thankful for the letter *m*. For she could be saved, because verse 26 says "not many noble" rather than "not any noble." Being wise, mighty, or noble may keep people from recognizing their need of the Savior. But when people come with a spirit of humility and inadequacy, God will save and use them.

The Despised

The word "despised" in verse 28 means "considered as nothing," while the phrase "things which are not" was a contemptible expression in the Greek language. Being ("material or immaterial existence") was everything to the Greeks, so being called a nothing was the worst kind of insult.

6. According to verses 29–31, why does God use the "weak" of the world for His purposes?

7. Read 1 Corinthians 2:1–5.
   (a) How does Paul describe himself?

   (b) Because of that, what did Paul's preaching demonstrate?

8. Many times in the Old Testament, God received glory by accomplishing His will through insignificant or "despised" things or people. Choose three of the following references to read. Then write down the examples from those passages.
   Exodus 4:2

   Numbers 22:32–33

Joshua 2:1–15

Judges 4:21

Judges 6:11–15

Judges 7:19–21

Any others you can think of?

Godly Wisdom

First Corinthians 2:5 refers to the opening discussion on faith. Our faith should not rest in a particular person or in ourselves! It is a demonstration of God's power. Likewise, true wisdom is not human wisdom, but God's.

9. Read 1 Corinthians 2:6–16.
   (a) In verses 7–8, what was the evidence that the Jewish rulers did not have the wisdom of God?

   (b) How does Paul describe the wisdom of God?

The world, even the Jewish religious leaders who denied Jesus, could not find true wisdom, because the wisdom of God, especially the mystery of the gospel, had been hidden.

10. Verse 9 is often quoted as referring to Heaven's mysteries, but in the context of verses 6–10, what is verse 9 actually referring to?

11. (a) According to 1 Corinthians 2:10, how does God reveal true wisdom to us?

    (b) When have you asked God for wisdom and the Holy Spirit gave it to you?

The Holy Spirit has several roles. In regard to the Scriptures, He worked in inspiration (2 Timothy 3:16; 2 Peter 1:20–21). Another role He plays is that of illuminator.

12. Look up the word *illumination* and write its definition.

The Holy Spirit takes the Word of God and enables us to understand it. He teaches us (1 Corinthians 2:10–13). However, the "natural" human, one without the Spirit of God, cannot discern the spiritual nature of the Word of God. The description "spiritual"—as opposed to "natural" or "sensual"—refers to the capacity of the redeemed (the saved and sanctified) to comprehend and discern God's truth.

13. Read 1 Corinthians 2:15. The Greek word for "judgeth" means "to scrutinize," "to ascertain." In the context of chapter 2, what does verse 15 mean?

14. What was something you did not understand before you received Jesus as your Savior but now that you are saved, you understand?

Application

First Corinthians 2 has shown a great dichotomy between the world and Christianity. The world values worldly wisdom, might, and power and therefore considers the gospel foolish. How do we apply the truths of 1 Corinthians 2?

First, we must understand that all we do for Christ may be considered foolishness to the world. How does that make you feel? Whose accolades are you looking for: the world's or Christ's? What passages of Scripture can you memorize and meditate on so you will look to serve Christ more than you look to be accepted by the world?

Second, we must understand that all we accomplish for Christ happens only in the power of the Holy Spirit. He is using our weak, earthen vessels to demonstrate God's power (2 Corinthians 4:7). Do you usually give glory to God, to Whom it is due? In other words, do you acknowledge His greatness, praise Him, and worship Him?

How does recognizing your need of the Holy Spirit's power demonstrate itself in your life? Do you go to God for strength, wisdom, and direction? A Christian woman who recognizes her dependency on Christ will start each day meeting with Him and asking for His wisdom and power to be evident.

Third, we must understand that no matter how weak, damaged, or despised we feel, God can use us! In fact, He will use us only when we come to the point of humbly acknowledging our weakness and allowing Him to work through us. Philippians

2:13 says, “For it is God which worketh in you both to will and to do of his good pleasure.” And 4:13 says, “I can do all things through Christ which strengtheneth me.” Be encouraged by the fact that God has chosen you to bear His name for His glory and that He is faithful (1 Corinthians 1:9). “Faithful is he that calleth you, who also will do it” (1 Thessalonians 5:28).

LESSON 3

Faithful Service

1 Corinthians 3:10—4:21

ONE OF THE RAPIDLY DEGENERATING Christian virtues today is faithfulness. Christians who once faithfully attended all services now find Sunday mornings sufficient for their busy lives. Many who once served in the church are now consumed with outside activities. The younger generations are growing up thinking that giving the Lord one hour on Sunday mornings, when convenient, is faithfulness.

Paul dedicates a good portion of 1 Corinthians to the importance of faithfulness. The local church cannot function without the faithfulness of its members. It is said that 10 percent of a church's members do 90 percent of the work. Are you part of that 10 percent or part of the 90?

Building Materials

In 1 Corinthians 3:10, Paul describes Christians' works for Christ as building on the foundation. Referring to verses 1–9, he reminds readers that one may lay the foundation and another may build upon that foundation. Lesson 2 reminded us that we are all part of the same team, laboring for the Lord, Who then gives the increase. A team needs all of its members to do their part, or the whole team suffers.

In this part of 1 Corinthians 3, Paul discusses the how and why of our building. The how is by taking heed to build things of eternal value on the foundation of Jesus Christ (vv. 10–11), and the why is for the glory of God (vv. 20–21).

1. Read 1 Corinthians 3:10–15.
   (a) What word do you see repeated in verses 13–15?

   (b) According to Ephesians 2:10, what does *work* refer to?

Though 1 Corinthians 3:10–15 may speak first of all to those who teach—that they are to be building on the foundation Paul laid in Jesus Christ—it is clear that this section also refers to the individual as it speaks about "any man" (v. 12) and "every man" (vv. 10, 13–15). We all "teach the gospel" by what we say and do. Not only do verses 13–15 refer to spiritual works, but they also assume we do them! The first question we must ask ourselves is whether we are doing any works for the Lord. Are we serving the Lord in the local church, or are we too busy with work, family, and outside interests? Before we can discuss the reason and manner we serve, we must examine what it is we actually do.

2. In 1 Corinthians 3:10–15, Paul uses building materials to compare our works for the Lord.
   (a) What are the six materials he mentions?

   (b) What determines their value?

3. What kind of works do these building materials represent?
   Gold, silver, precious stones

   Wood, hay, stubble

Notice that all can be used as building materials and are not worthless in the temporal realm. But when tested by fire, only half of them have eternal value. We need to examine how we spend our lives: how much of what we do has eternal value?

4. Read Matthew 6:19–21, 25–34. What is the priority named in verse 33?

When you read those verses and think of your life, is that your priority? Too often we are so concerned about meeting our physical needs that we do not think about advancing the kingdom of God.

5. In 1 Corinthians 3:14, Paul speaks of rewards for "any man's work." These will be given at the Judgment Seat of Christ, where believers are rewarded for their service to Christ (2 Corinthians 5:10). Though we don't know what kind of reward Paul is referring to, other Scriptures refer to rewards as crowns. Look up the following verses and write down the reward and the reason for it.

   1 Corinthians 9:24–25

   2 Timothy 4:8

   James 1:12; Revelation 2:10

   1 Peter 5:1–4

6. According to Revelation 4:10, what will we do with these rewards?

Oh, to have something to give back! We come to eternity owing everything to the Lamb, Who died for us. I so want to have something to give to Him!

Read 1 Corinthians 3:16–17. In speaking of the "temple of God" in verse 16, Paul is referring to the church rather than the individual. In this context, we are building together as a local body, but if anyone defiles the church, God will destroy that person. Verse 17 is a strong warning to anyone who is trying to undermine a church's ministry. If you defile a church, God will destroy you!

The Required Thing

How can any service we perform be discounted eternally? What determines whether we receive a reward for our labor?

7. Read 1 Corinthians 3:18–23. According to these verses, how might someone be building with wood, hay, or stubble and lose his or her reward?

Moving into 1 Corinthians 4, the word "ministers" or "servants" in verse 1 is different from the one in 3:5. The word in 4:1 is the Greek word *huperetes,* which literally meant "under rowers." It referred to the lowest galley slaves, the ones rowing on the bottom tier of a ship. Since they were the lowest of the slaves, the term came to refer to subordinates or ones under authority. Paul refers to himself as the lowest of the slaves of Christ yet also a steward. A steward was a house manager.

8. According to 4:1–2, what else is required as Christians serve?

Faithfulness in a steward is the one thing required. God does not require brilliance, great talents, or perfection as we serve Him. Only faithfulness. Our work for the Lord becomes wood, hay, and stubble when we lack faithfulness.

9. (a) What meanings for *faithfulness* can you find in a dictionary?

   (b) How would you describe faithfulness in a servant of Christ and a steward of the mysteries of God?

For Christians, faithfulness requires staying true to the Scriptures and guarding that truth, being loyal to a local church, serving in that local church, and being responsible and reliable in that service. The description "strict in the performance of a duty" includes being faithful in attendance and in being on time for the commitments we have made. It means others can count on us to follow through in our commitments. In character, faithfulness means that our lives consistently depict the character of Christ and the fruit of the Spirit.

10. Read 1 Corinthians 4:3–5. Here Paul touches on motivation. We cannot know why someone serves, whether for self-glory or God's glory, but God knows the heart.

    (a) What will God make manifest, or obvious, according to verse 5?

    (b) What will be the result?

In 1 Corinthians 4:6–21 Paul gives examples of the requirements for reward. He reminds the Corinthians first of all not to look at people or their abilities, which causes division.

11. Paul confronts an attitude he sees in the church at Corinth (vv. 6–7). What is that attitude?

12. In verse 7, what does he remind believers of? (Hint: The phrase "who maketh thee to differ" could mean "who regards you as superior.")

It would seem that the Corinthians thought they had it all together and were smug in their self-righteousness. Verse 8 is written sarcastically and could be worded this way: "No doubt you are already full, already rich, and reigning as kings without our help." Paul then compares their air of superiority with the degrading and distressing lives of the apostles.

13. In verses 9–16, Paul gives the example of the apostles' faithfulness to the ministry no matter the obstacles.
    (a) According to verse 9, what were the apostles made?

    (b) What does that mean?

14. According to verses 11–13, what were some of the things the apostles suffered in their ministry while remaining faithful?

15. In 2 Corinthians 11:23–28 Paul lists some of the things he had suffered personally. What does he list?

How many of us have suffered even a fraction of what Paul suffered? He served faithfully, never giving up and always following through. When we think of Paul's example, how do our excuses for not serving faithfully hold up?

"I have to get up early every other day; Sunday is my day to sleep in."

"My kids have soccer [or T-ball or play practice or band practice or . . .], so I won't be able to attend Sunday nights for a while. "

"Sorry I wasn't here last Sunday but I had family visiting."

"I know the songs. I don't need to get to practice on time."

"Work day? I have too much work at my own house!"

I could address every one of these excuses individually, but every one of them comes down to priorities. We probably wouldn't use any of these excuses for being late or absent from work! When Christ is not our first priority, there will always be things that come ahead of our service to Him.

16. Another example of faithfulness is given in verse 17. Who is that example?

Application

Timothy, a disciple of Paul, had obviously been well instructed by his mentor. Paul called him "faithful" and trusted Timothy to carry his message to the church. "Trustworthy" can be substituted for the word "faithful" in 4:2.

So how do we measure up when we think of this area of faithful service, or works? First, are you serving the Lord in your local church? Are you part of that 10 percent who enable the church to function, or are you part of the 90 percent who watch others serve? If you serve, how much time do you dedicate to serving the Lord?

Second, what is the motivation for your service? Everything we do should be for God's glory and for His church. If vainglory or a self-serving attitude enters in, our work is wood, hay, or stubble and will be revealed at the Judgment Seat of Christ.

Third, are you faithful in the things God has called you to do? Is your work for the Lord a priority? Can people count on you to follow through? Are you on time as a teacher, a nursery worker, a choir member, or an attender? When you fail in your responsibilities, others are always affected. Be faithful!

Last, teach your children the importance of serving the Lord faithfully. For the church to remain strong, the next generation must serve faithfully.

There is nothing more discouraging to leadership in the church than a lack of faithfulness, yet we are seeing it more and more in our churches today. We need to pray that our churches would be filled with faithful servants, slaves of Christ, where 90 percent of the membership, rather than 10 percent, are involved in furthering the gospel and using their gifts for His glory.

LESSON 4

Dealing with Sin

1 Corinthians 5:1—6:8

BEFORE I EVEN OPENED THE LETTER, I knew it couldn't be good. My sister never wrote letters. In fact, she had been pulling away from communication with the family the last few years. As I began to read, I wept. My sister had decided she was gay and was in a "committed relationship" with a woman she had previously introduced as a good friend—a good Christian friend. My sister's choice would change the dynamics of all of our family relationships as we each processed this information and prayed as to how to handle this sin Biblically.

Paul addressed a similar situation in his first letter to the Corinthians. He closed chapter 4 asking whether he would need to go to Corinth "with a rod." He then addressed the immorality happening in the church and the church's refusal to deal with it.

A Stain on the Name of Christ

1. In 1 Corinthians 5 what sin was Paul confronting in the church of Corinth (v. 1)?

While the English word is *fornication,* the Greek word is *porneia,* from which we get *pornography.* It refers to any illicit sexual activity.

2. (a) Read Leviticus 18:7–8, 29; Deuteronomy 22:30. What did the Old Testament law say about this sin?

   (b) What was the penalty?

3. Going back to our text in 1 Corinthians 5, how had the church responded to this sin (v. 2)?

Paul said that this sin was "reported commonly." What a stain on the name of Christ as well as on the name of the Corinthian church! Everyone knew about this sin, but nothing was being done. Even the unsaved (the Gentiles) would have been ashamed of this sin.

Though the sin of immorality brings a stain to the church, it is far worse when a church tries to hide it or doesn't deal with it. We have seen that truth today, as the media has strong condemnation for any religious group that tries to protect one of its own by covering that person's sin, especially when the sin is illegal. The sin of incest was strictly forbidden under Roman law, yet the church was not dealing with it.

4. In 1 Corinthians 5:3–5, what did Paul command regarding this individual?

5. What do you think the Corinthians thought "deliver . . . unto Satan" means? (See also 1 Timothy 1:20.)

6. Explain the result of being "delivered unto Satan," according to verse 5.

Obviously, not all physical ailments or death are divine judgment. Most result from living in a sinful world with its natural consequences. However, Paul reminded the Corinthians a few chapters later that some among them were sickly and some "slept" due to sin in their lives. Hebrews 12:4–11 makes it clear that the Lord chastens, or disciplines, those He loves.

Withdrawing Fellowship

7. What example does Paul use in 1 Corinthians 5:6–8 to show the results of allowing sin in the church? Explain the comparison.

Throughout Scripture, leaven is most often used as a symbol of influence (usually evil), such as in 1 Corinthians 5:8; Matthew 16:6; Galatians 5:9. Leaven permeates a loaf of bread to cause it to rise. In the church, allowing sin to continue can permeate the whole church. Leaven also represented the old life. When the Israelites left Egypt, they took unleavened bread. They were leaving behind their old life and entering a new one. Passover, which celebrated the sacrifice of the lamb that gave protection from the death angel, was always followed by the Feast of Unleavened Bread, in which all leaven was removed from the house. The Passover Lamb, Christ, has shed His blood and saved us from death. Now we are to remove the leaven from our lives and walk in holiness.

8. (a) What command did Paul give the church about how to treat this fornicator (vv. 9–11)?

   (b) Explain what you think that means in real-life practice.

What differentiation does Paul make in these verses; in other words, whom specifically does this command apply to?

Paul made clear that believers are not to avoid contact with the unsaved; we need to win them! His command applies to our treatment of a professing Christian whose behavior is shaming the name of Christ. In other words, it is improper to have fellowship with someone who is unrepentant and under discipline.

John MacArthur, in his commentary on 1 Corinthians, writes,

> Faithful believers are not to keep close company with any fellow believers who persistently practice serious sins such as those mentioned here. If the offenders will not listen to the counsel and warning of two or three other believers and not even of the whole church they are to be put out of the fellowship.... They should be totally cut off both from individual and corporate fellowship with other Christians, including that of eating together. No exceptions are made. Even if the unrepentant person is a close friend or family member, he is to be put out.

The same instructions as we saw in chapter 1 are given regarding those causing division. Second Thessalonians 3:6 and 14 say to "withdraw yourselves from every brother that walketh disorderly" (v. 6) and "have no company with them" (v. 14).

This may seem harsh, but God desires holiness in His Bride (the church), and He will protect her at all costs.

9. After reading Matthew 18:15–17, describe the process of church discipline.

Step 1: The offended person ______________________.

Step 2: If the offender doesn't repent / make it right, ______________________.

Step 3: If the offender still doesn't repent / make it right, ______________________.

Step 4: If the offender doesn't listen to the church, ______________________________.

10. According to 2 Corinthians 7:8–12, how did the church respond to the harshness of Paul's words?

When my sister made her life choice, my husband and I wrestled with 1 Corinthians 5. She is a Christian but was not part of any local church; she had stopped attending when she started heading toward this sinful lifestyle. So how were we to respond? Is this passage just for those attending the same church? In the New Testament church, most cities would have had multiple house churches. So did this apply to those in the same "house church"?

My sister lived states away, so what was our responsibility? Some in the family applied this passage only to "church" discipline (of which there wasn't any). So, other than confronting her and voicing their displeasure, there were no other consequences. If someone is disciplined by one church, what is the responsibility of the other churches in the area? Can the one in sin just go to the church a few miles away and join? Does this command apply only to the church that person is a member of or to the Body of Christ in general?

Based on 1 Corinthians 5:9–11, we decided that we could not "keep company" with my sister, whom I love. I also decided that keeping in touch through Facebook or any other social media is another form of fellowship and decided to cut those ties. It was the hardest decision of my life, but honoring and obeying the Word of God is my first priority, even when many in the family took a different stand. If there are no consequences to a sinful lifestyle, if everyone treats you the same, then sorrow unto repentance (2 Corinthians 7:10) will be hindered. Be careful not to criticize those who, in trying to follow God, make the difficult decision to have no fellowship with someone in sin. Though you may not agree with them, they are not unloving; they are trying to follow Biblical teaching according to their conscience.

11. What does Paul say in verses 12–13 is the church's responsibility?

A common saying in Christian circles today is "Don't judge!" However, God has commanded us to judge and discern sin within the church and to deal with it! Every one of us commits sin and needs to confess and repent every day. However, when a Christian's lifestyle shames Christ and that Christian is unrepentant, the church's responsibility is to deal with it Biblically.

Taking Other Christians to Court

Read 1 Corinthians 6:1–8.

12. What sin does Paul deal with in these verses?

13. Read Matthew 19:28 and 1 Corinthians 6:2–3. In Corinthians 6:2, what does "the saints shall judge the world" mean?

14. Paul gives two alternate ways to deal with the issues rather than going to court. What are they?

Application

Church discipline is Biblical and necessary, yet we are seeing less and less of it in today's "tolerance" culture. The cultural view of total acceptance has crept into the church, and many leaders hesitate to confront sin. In many megachurches, there is no accountability at all for one's lifestyle, simply due to the number of members.

So what can we do? First, guard your heart! Walk closely with God so you do not become the "leaven" that needs to be purged from the church.

Second, when Biblical church discipline is necessary, support your leadership in this very difficult decision. Do not be the one that criticizes the person trying to do what is right according to Scripture. Discipline is not something that any pastor enjoys.

Third, uphold the discipline in your own personal practice. Do not have fellowship with the one under discipline. This means that eating out, shopping, or just hanging out with that person is no longer possible.

Finally, remember that the goal is restoration. The person in sin needs your prayers! If you do happen to run into that person, express your love and say you are praying for him or her. My church has seen members restored to our church through Biblical discipline and prayer.

Christ desires to present the church to Himself as a bride without spot or wrinkle (Ephesians 5:25–27). We also, with the heart of God, need to value holiness in our lives as well as in our church.

LESSON 5

Bought with a Price

1 Corinthians 6:9–20

WHEN WE LOOK AT SOCIETY TODAY, we marvel at the degradation—and the acceptance of it. Things that shocked people twenty years ago are now announced proudly. Could Paul possibly understand what we deal with in today's world? Yes, he could! The society that surrounded the Corinthian church was probably as bad, or worse, than what we see today.

Corinth was known for its temple to Aphrodite with its one thousand prostitutes. The Greek word *korinthiazomai,* which is interpreted "to act the Corinthian," means "to practice fornication." Along with this, homosexuality and other sexual perversions were prevalent among the Greeks and Romans. Many of the Greek philosophers and Roman emperors practiced homosexuality. There is nothing new under the sun!

Paul needed to remind the Corinthian believers that they were to be different from the culture around them. They had been bought by the blood of Christ and belonged to Him. No matter what is accepted in popular culture today, our lives should be governed by Biblical culture.

Washed, Sanctified, Justified

1. In 1 Corinthians 6:9–10, Paul lists those who will not be part of the kingdom of God. It is interesting to note that he doesn't list the sin, such as fornication, but the person, a fornicator. This word choice indicates a lifestyle rather

than a onetime sin. From this passage, list the type of person named and the meaning behind the title. Use a Bible dictionary, concordance, or commentary if necessary.

Word	Refers to

2. Paul states that those whose lives exhibit wickedness will not inherit the kingdom of God. How can he say that? See Matthew 7:16–20; Mark 7:20–23; Galatians 5:19–24.

The next statement in 1 Corinthians 6:11 is one of hope and rejoicing: "And such *were* some of you" (italics added). Christ can change anyone! No matter what sinful lifestyle a person may be enslaved to, there is freedom in Christ.

3. In verse 11 Paul describes with three words what has happened to the believers in Corinth. What are they?

4. Using the cross-references given below, write a definition of each term:
   Washed (John 13:10; Titus 3:3–5; Revelation 1:5)

   Sanctified (John 17:17–19; 1 Corinthians 1:2; Hebrews 10:10–14)

   Justified (Romans 3:24–28; 4:1–8; 5:1)

5. As mentioned in lesson 1, the three aspects of sanctification are positional (past), progressive (present), and perfect (future). In positional sanctification we are saved from the penalty of sin (Romans 8:1). In progressive sanctification we are being saved from the power of sin and becoming more like Christ (Romans 6:12; 8:29). In perfect sanctification we will be saved from the presence of sin! How are these three stages laid out in 1 John 3:1–3?

Sexual Sins

In 1 Corinthians 6:12–13, Paul introduces a subject that will be covered in lesson 7. Several commentators suggest that the statement "all things are lawful" was actually a common saying in that day, excusing sinful behavior. Some in the church may have been using Christian freedom to justify their sin. Paul lists two considerations that would limit their freedom: Is it expedient ("helpful")? And will it enslave? The saying "meats for the belly" was being used to justify immorality. Just as meats ("food") and the belly go together in God's creation, so the body and sex go together.

6. How does Paul answer that argument in verse 13?

7. Read 1 Corinthians 6:15–18. Paul explains that fornication for a Christian involves the Lord. How does Paul describe it in these verses?

8. Verse 18 starts with a command: flee fornication! Read Genesis 39:7–12. How is this command pictured in real life?

9. Verse 18 goes on to say, “He that committeth fornication sinneth against his own body.” How would you explain that statement?

10. Read the following verses and write what they say about sexual sins.
    1 Thessalonians 4:3–5

    Proverbs 5:3–12

    Proverbs 6:32–35

    Ephesians 5:3

Temples of God

First Corinthians 6:19–20 concludes this section with two wonderful statements. The first one is that the Holy Spirit resides within us! If we could keep this truth foremost in our minds, we might think twice before we sin. For when we sin, we drag God into our sin. Each of us is His temple, and that temple should be pure.

The second statement is that we are "bought with a price." Christ has bought us back from the slave market and set us free—exactly what the word *redemption* means.

11. Read 1 Peter 1:18–19. What are we redeemed with?

12. According to 1 Corinthians 6:20, since we believers have been bought with a price, what is our responsibility?

13. What does the word *glorify* mean?

Application

Our world has the same problem as Paul's world—a glorification of sex outside of marriage. God created sex to be a beautiful union between husband and wife, yet our culture has demeaned it to simple fleshly gratification between any two people, no matter the gender. Romans 1:26–28 describes the world today; and I'm afraid that verse 28 is being fulfilled, where "God gave them over to a reprobate mind, to do those things which are not [right]."

So how should you respond?

First, protect your mind. Television programs, movies, books, and other media are subtly making perversions normal.

A number of regular TV programs feature homosexuality, and countless movies also include scenes dedicated to the practice. We become conformed to the world through our minds (Romans 12:2). Instead of filling your mind with garbage, keep your mind on things that are true, pure, and lovely (Philippians 4:8).

Second, remember Who dwells within you, and do not grieve Him by what you do.

Third, be thankful! God paid a precious price for you! As believers, we have been bought from the slave market to freedom in Christ. We should be a very grateful people.

Last, let all you do cause others to think more highly of your God. Philippians 1:20–21 are my life verses. They are a prayer that God would be magnified in my body by life or death. *To magnify* means "to make bigger." I want people to see God in a bigger way when they view my life. I hope that is your prayer too.

LESSON 6

God's View of Marriage and Singleness

1 Corinthians 7

THREE MEN HAD COME TO VISIT Paul in Ephesus, possibly bringing a letter from the church at Corinth with them (1 Corinthians 16:17). The next few chapters of 1 Corinthians were written by Paul in response to a letter—possibly that letter (1 Corinthians 7:1).

The Corinthians' first question related to marriage and singleness. Roman law allowed for four types of marriage:

- If slaves wanted to be married, they were allowed to live together in what would have been termed "tent companionship." But if their master decided to sell one of them or simply changed his mind, he had that right.
- Another form was common-law marriage, like we have today. If a couple lived together for a year, they were recognized as husband and wife.
- A father might sell his daughter to a prospective husband.
- People of the nobility were married in a ceremony similar to what we see today. The ceremony was eventually adopted by the Catholic Church and came into Protestantism through the Reformation. It included the participation of both

> families, someone to stand up for the bride (present-day maid of honor) and for the groom (best man), exchanging of vows, wearing a veil, and the giving of a ring. However, divorce was common, and some nobles were married twenty times or more.[1]

The Corinthian church may have had members living together under any of these conditions. But becoming a Christian meant a total change in their view of marriage. They would have had questions about marriage versus singleness, level of commitment, living with an unbeliever, and more. Paul answers these questions in 1 Corinthians 7. Again, Biblical truths always supersede culture. Even as our society moves farther and farther away from God's ideal for marriage, we need to stand firmly on what the Word of God teaches us.

Paul addresses two callings and three issues in this chapter. The two callings are marriage and singleness. Within those callings he addresses the issues of sexual relations in marriage, stability in marriage, and support for singleness.

God may call you to marriage or singleness. Neither calling is to be disdained or held as inferior. Our calling is determined by our walk with God day by day and allowing Him to lead. Whether we decide to marry or remain single, we are not to ignore the Biblical guidelines.

Read 1 Corinthians 7:1–9. In the first couple of verses, Paul encourages those who have strong sexual desire to marry. Typically, men have a much stronger sex drive than women. It would be difficult for a man created with a strong sex drive to remain single and not commit fornication. In verses 1–2 and 8–9, Paul encourages marriage for those who struggle to be self-disciplined in the area of sexual drive. The remainder of this section is dedicated to the marital relationship.

---

[1] John MacArthur, *The Divorce Dilemma: God's Last Word on Lasting Commitment* (Leominster, England: Day One Publications, 2009), 59–60.

Sexual Relations in Marriage

1. If God has led someone to marriage, what are spouses to render to each other, according to verse 3?

2. A principle in verse 4 drives the practical application in verse 3. What is that principle?

3. Paul uses the word *defraud* in verse 5. What does that word mean?

4. What does verse 5 say is the only condition for sexual abstinence in marriage?

You may be thinking that you need to pray and fast more often! Just remember that abstinence is a mutual decision and is set "for a time."

5. Why is it import that abstinence lasts for only a set period of time, then the couple comes together again?

Stability in Marriage

In the next section of chapter 7, Paul deals with stability in marriage, or the permanence of marriage. Read 1 Corinthians 7:10–24 and 39–40.

6. What is Paul's first command in this passage (vv. 10–11)?

7. Read Mark 10:1–12 and summarize the passage.

8. A unique situation is presented in 1 Corinthians 7:12–16. What is that situation?

As Christianity spread, most likely there were many divided households. The Corinthians may have questioned whether they should stay married to an unbeliever immersed in paganism. Paul addressed this situation with these new Christians, encouraging them to do all they could to remain with an unbelieving spouse. Marriage vows are sacred, and God's perfect will is always permanence in marriage.

9. (a) How does staying with an unbeliever benefit the home, according to verse 14?

   (b) What does that mean? (Hint: See 1 Peter 3:1–6.)

In 1 Corinthians 7:15–16, Paul addresses the situation in which the unbeliever decides to leave. Although believers are never to pursue divorce, sometimes the unbelieving spouse refuses to stay. These believers are advised to let the unbelieving spouse go. Verses 15–16 are taken by some to mean that believers are then free to remarry, using the words "not under bondage" as their reasoning. These verses should not be interpreted apart from all the other teachings on divorce and remarriage, so we are going to do a brief overview of those New Testament Scriptures. Second, we will look at the word *bondage.*

In several Scriptures, Christ addresses the issues of divorce and remarriage. Paul says in 1 Corinthians 7:10–11 that divorced people are not to remarry. Verse 39 states that a wife is bound to her husband as long as he lives. No exceptions are given in those verses.

10. Paul states this principle in Romans 7:1–3 as well. Summarize these verses.

These verses state clearly that a married person is to remain with his or her spouse as long as the two live: "until death do us part." There are no exceptions given in these verses or in 1 Corinthians 7:39.

11. In question 7, we looked at a passage in Mark 10. Read the parallel passages in Matthew 5:31–32; 19:3–9; Luke 16:18. What do you see in the Matthew passages that are not included in the Mark and Luke accounts?

Why does one Gospel include an exception clause and not the others? Are the Scriptures inconsistent? To understand this addition, we need to understand the audience for each of the Gospels.

Matthew was written primarily to the Jews to answer their questions about Jesus of Nazareth, Who claimed to be their Messiah. Christ is introduced as the King of the Jews. The book of Mark emphasizes Jesus as a servant and was written primarily for Gentile readers. The book of Luke introduces Jesus as the Son of Man and was written for the Greeks. The purpose of the book of John was to confirm the deity of Jesus Christ, as stated in John 20:30–31.

The exception clause is included only in the book of

Matthew, which was written to the Jews. The word used for *fornication* there is the Greek word *porneuo,* meaning "to act the harlot." This word is primarily used in Scripture for sex before marriage. Notice that Matthew did not use the word translated "adultery" in most passages. That would be the Greek word *moichos,* which means exactly that, "to commit adultery, or to be apostate" (spiritual adultery). Why would Matthew talk about getting a divorce from someone who committed "fornication," or sex before marriage, instead of adultery?

12. Read Matthew 1:18–20. What was Joseph considering because of Mary's condition?

13. (a) What word in verse 19 identifies Joseph?

    (b) Were Mary and Joseph married at this point?

The Jewish law considered betrothal, the engagement period, seriously. A couple were called husband and wife though the ceremony had not yet taken place. To break an engagement, a writing of divorce was required. The betrothal could be broken and a divorce could take place if one of the two was unfaithful during this period. The divorce was a necessary part of breaking the betrothal.

Since Matthew is written to the Jews, the exception clause is included, using the word *fornication,* because they had a right to divorce their betrothed for unfaithfulness. They had not yet come together as husband and wife and were not one flesh at this point. The exception clause would be applicable only when writing to the Jewish people, because the Gentile people did not require a divorce to end a betrothal; therefore, Mark and Luke would not need to include it. Even if you believe this is an exception clause for divorce from a spouse, there is still no permission given for remarriage.

Therefore, since all the other New Testament Scriptures teach that remarriage after divorce is adultery, the fact that the unbelieving spouse has left and the believing spouse is "not under bondage" do not mean the believer is free to remarry. That would contradict all other Scriptures. Though the exception clause is subject to debate among scholars, it seems that this no-remarriage view is the most consistent with the rest of Scripture.

Second, the word translated "bondage" in 1 Corinthians 7:15 is different from the word in 7:39 translated "bound." The word *bondage* is from the Greek word *douloo,* which means "servant" or "slave." *Bound* in verse 39 comes from the Greek word *deo,* meaning "tied." That is the word Paul used in Romans 7:1–2 as well as in 1 Corinthians 7:27. A wife or husband is "tied" to her or his spouse until death.

If an unbelieving spouse leaves, the believer is not required to "make it work." The believing spouse does all he or she can, then demonstrates peaceful submission. The believer is not a slave to the marriage.

Ephesians 5 shows marriage as a picture of Christ and the church. That Biblical picture is getting more and more distorted every day as Christianity begins to accept divorce as normal for the followers of Christ.

Read 1 Corinthians 7:17–24 and 27. In these verses Paul urges the Corinthians to stay in the situation they were in when they were saved. The word translated "called" through these verses refers to their salvation. Obviously, they needed to make changes if they were living a sinful lifestyle, but there was confusion in the church in Corinth as to what this "new life" meant in the areas of marriage and singleness.

14. What three examples did Paul give to the church to remain the same?

Support for Singleness

Read 1 Corinthians 7:25–40. Paul desired that whether married or single, each believer would have a single focus: serving Christ.

15. According to verses 32–35, what advantage is there to being single in the church?

In Jewish culture, fathers had a dominant role in whom their daughters married. In verses 36–38, Paul addresses the fathers who made this decision for their daughters. If they believed that their daughters should remain single, that was fine. But as a daughter passed "the flower of her age," she might have desired marriage; she might not have had the gift of singleness (yes, it is a gift). Either one was good—to give a daughter in marriage or to have her remain single.

16. Reread verses 39–40. What are Paul's last words of wisdom on this subject?

Application

After studying 1 Corinthians 7, how should you respond?

First, choose wisely! Knowing that God ordained marriage to be "until death do us part," do not rush into any relationship. Prayerfully and carefully let the Lord lead you.

Second, do everything you can to protect your marriage, including being available to your husband to meet his sexual needs. This passage makes it clear that it is a requirement in marriage, not an option. Though this study doesn't expound on it, our intimate relations should also be a privilege and joy as we meet the needs of the man we love.

Third, if God has allowed you to be single, rejoice in the opportunities you have to be used by Him. Singleness is not a curse or a punishment from God. Is your focus on getting a husband? Or is it on serving and pleasing Christ? As my mom used to say, "Life isn't about finding the right person; it's about being the right person."

Maybe your marriage has already failed and you are facing decisions about remarriage. Study the Scriptures and decide based on truth, not emotions. Know what you believe and why. It's easy to have strong convictions until you or someone you love is placed in that situation.

Finally, be careful how you view singles. As women, we are often quick to be matchmakers for our single friends instead of encouraging them in their singleness. As a church, we should reach out to the singles among us, not to fix them up, but to include them in our families and church activities.

Some are quick to support remarriage after divorce because no one, they say, should have to be alone. Is singleness a punishment? Maybe when we view singleness as a gift, we will view remarriage in a different light.

God has ordained both marriage and singleness. Instead of trying to change the situation we are in, let us use whichever gift He has given us to glorify Him.

LESSON 7

Lawful but Loving

1 Corinthians 8; 10:14–33

ONE OF THE MOST DIVISIVE ISSUES in Christianity today are the gray areas. Many practices are not specifically forbidden in Scripture or spelled out in black and white. In those areas, Christians must rely on discernment, their conscience, and the leading of the Holy Spirit. God knows what is pleasing and glorifying to Him—there is nothing gray to Him. Therefore, as mature Christians, we seek His mind regarding questionable practices.

It would seem that the Corinthian church struggled with the same issue, especially in the practice of eating meat that had been offered to idols. Paul addressed that specific issue, then he gave a principle for our practice: loving over lawful.

To understand the issue, we must understand what was involved in pagan worship. Both the Greeks and Romans believed that demons were constantly trying to enter humans and would attach themselves to food before it was eaten. The only way to rid the demons from the food was to offer it as a sacrifice. This served a twofold purpose: getting rid of the demons in the food and offering sacrifices in worship.

Part of meat offered as a sacrifice was burned to the god; part of it was given to the priest as payment; and the remainder was left to the worshiper. The priests often had far more meat than they could eat, so they would sell it in the marketplace. That meat was highly valued, since it had been "cleansed" of the demons.

Besides the marketplace, most festivals, marriages, and so

forth were held in the pagan temple, and the food served would most certainly be food that had been offered to idols. Some of the Gentile believers refused to eat such food, because it reminded them of their pagan past or because they didn't want others to think they believed in the demonic possession of the food. Some of the Jewish believers, though not from that background, considered that meat unclean for them to eat. But many of the Christians had no problem with the meat, understanding that pagan deities did not exist and evil spirits did not contaminate the food. This had become a source of contention in the church and had resulted in arrogance on the part of some.

Principle: Love before Knowledge

Read 1 Corinthians 8. Paul first addresses those Christians who feel superior in their knowledge—the knowledge that idols are not real and the food sacrificed to them is just food. They had become arrogant, looking down on the believers who were uncomfortable about eating food that had once been offered to idols.

1. (a) What two things does Paul compare in verse 1?

   (b) What does he say about each?

2. According to verse 2, what does a man of knowledge need to acknowledge?

3. Instead of being known for our intellect, what should believers desire to be known for (v. 3)?

Read Romans 14:1–12. This passage deals with the same issue in the Roman church.

4. What two areas of conviction are being discussed in verses 2 and 5?

Besides the issue of eating meat offered to idols, there was also the question of which holy days and feasts should be observed after someone came to Christ.

5. What are the keys for dealing with such issues, according to Romans 14:5–6?
   Verse 5

   Verse 6

6. What does Paul conclude in Romans 14:3–4 and 10 about how to treat someone with different convictions?

7. In 1 Corinthians 8:4–6, Paul gives some basic teaching. Summarize his message to the Corinthian church.

Paul reminds the church in verse 7 that not all believers have this knowledge. Many times people are saved out of difficult spiritual backgrounds. Some practices may simply trigger memories and emotions that are hard to handle. It may be that believers know the truth but that the association is still there, stirring up what they've tried to leave behind. They may be sensitive to things that others don't think twice about. Instead of disdaining their feelings, we need to respond with love and understanding.

8. According to 1 Corinthians 8:8, who is the more spiritual of the two: the knowledgeable brother or the weak brother?

Principle: Love over Freedom

9. Paul gives a warning about our Christian liberty in verse 9. What is it?

10. Read verses 10–12 and Romans 14:13–21 and explain what a stumbling block is.

In Romans 14:15, Paul uses the words "if thy brother be grieved," then you are not walking in love. Not every stumbling block causes a brother to sin—it may cause a brother to grieve. When you have a strong conviction about an activity and see others do it without a thought, it is a grief to your spirit.

11. Paul makes a strong statement in 1 Corinthians 8:12 about using knowledge and freedom even when it hurts a fellow Christian. What does Paul call it?

12. In 1 Corinthians 10:23, Paul says all things are lawful but that not all things are expedient or edify. Also see 1 Corinthians 6:12. How would you explain this concept?

Paul's directives in this matter are found in 1 Corinthians 8:13 and 10:14–33. In chapter 8, Paul says he will abstain totally from meat if eating it causes a brother to stumble. In chapter 10, he gives specifics regarding various situations a Corinthian believer could find him- or herself in regarding this issue of eating meat.

Read 1 Corinthians 10:14–22. Here Paul first addresses the issue of the festivals taking place in the pagan temple. Paul compares the communion of the Lord's Supper to a similar connection in taking part in a pagan feast.

13. In verses 16–17, the word translated "communion" means "partnership" or "partaking." What do you think Paul is trying to say in these verses?

When Israelites offered sacrifices on the altar in the Old Testament, they were active participants in the offering in worship and fellowship with God (1 Corinthians 10:18).

14. (a) Should the Corinthian believers have taken part in idol feasts?

    (b) What was Paul's conclusion, found in verses 19–21?

Next Paul gave a command and practical applications of that command (1 Corinthians 10:24–30). The command is to seek the welfare of others before yourself. We looked at a similar command in Philippians 2:2–4: be like-minded, esteem others better than yourself, and don't look at your own things, but look on the things of others.

15. In verses 25–28 how does Paul suggest the Corinthian believers handle the issue of eating meat in the situations mentioned?

Application

Paul's conclusion is given in verse 31. Whatever we do—eat, drink, or anything else—should be for God's glory. This is the overriding motivation for all we do. When the motivation becomes our own glory or fulfilling our own desires, it becomes sin—whether it's lawful or not.

Paul cites his own example in 10:32—11:1. Just as Paul sought to seek the profit of others over himself and to never offend, he encouraged the Corinthian church to follow him in that lofty goal.

We hear a lot about "legalistic Christians"—sometimes just because they have stronger convictions than others. The term *legalistic,* explained chiefly in the book of Galatians, has to do with an insistence by Jews that everyone had to keep aspects of the Jewish law, even after converting to Christianity, or the person was not truly saved. Paul rebuked these Jews in Galatians 2:16, saying that no one is justified by keeping the law, but by faith in Christ. Abstaining from something as a conviction does not make someone legalistic—perhaps it makes him or her more discerning! The "weaker" brother was weak due to a lack of knowledge. If a mature Christian differs from you in conviction, it would not be from a lack of knowledge, but it could possibly be from a greater understanding of God's holiness. Be careful in using the term *legalistic.*

As we face decisions regarding those gray areas, ask yourself three questions:

First, is it really a gray area? Have I searched the Scriptures and sought God's mind about this? Read the Word and pray, asking God for mature discernment.

Second, is this profitable to me rather than harmful? If it could harm your body, your mind, or your emotions, it is not God's will. If it has no profit at all, that may be another clue that you should abstain from it.

Third, will this freedom cause another believer to stumble or grieve? If so, you need to abstain from that practice in that believer's presence or abstain altogether.

If anything is so important to you that you don't care what others think, it is an idol. God wants us to care what others think! Offending other believers does not glorify Him.

Knowing the freedom you have in Christ—freedom from the law—should give you great joy. But you should also realize that your ultimate purpose is to glorify Christ and edify others. Love always trumps liberty.

LESSON 8

Our Spiritual Leaders

1 Corinthians 9

MY HUSBAND AND I have been in ministry together for over thirty-eight years—in the same church! We have seen great blessing and great disappointment. Some of our people have shown amazing faithfulness, encouraging us greatly. But others' commitment to the church has waned; some have abandoned their faith; and a few have even tried to destroy the church.

In 2 Corinthians 11:23–28 Paul lists the trials and sufferings he has gone through. The last thing he mentions is something that burdened him daily—the care of the churches. When someone is in ministry, the church's burdens become his burdens, their joys become his joys, and their failures become his failures. The people of the church are his family, and ministry is his life. If not for the grace of God, very few would stay in ministry. But serving the King of Kings also gives great joy, even in the midst of trials.

As we look at the issue of spiritual leadership, examine your attitude toward your pastor, your support of him, and your own faithfulness to your local church.

In 1 Corinthians 9, Paul illustrates from his own life the principle taught in chapter 8. We may sometimes need to set aside our "rights" for the good of the Body and the spread of the gospel. Paul first establishes his apostolic position and privileges. Then he shows how he practiced this principle of love over liberty while reminding the Corinthian church of their responsibility to those who shepherded them.

A Minister's Rights

Read 1 Corinthians 9:1–14. In verse 1, Paul reminds the Corinthian believers that he was an apostle and had the freedom found in Christ.

1. What mark of an apostle is seen in verse 1? (See also 1 Corinthians 15:7–10.)

2. Paul refers to the Corinthians as what two things in verses 1–2?

Paul then questioned the church as to his rights as an apostle and a preacher of the gospel.

3. What three rights ("powers") does Paul talk about in verses 4–6?

The apostles should not have had to think about where their next meal was coming from while they traveled and ministered. Many of the other apostles were married, as were Christ's brothers. Paul was saying that the church had a responsibility to support the apostles' ministry, even if it meant supporting a wife and family as well.

4. Verse 7 gives three examples of those that derive their living from their occupation. What are those examples?

Paul then quotes the Old Testament law in verse 9. Deuteronomy 25:4 says, "Thou shalt not muzzle the ox when he treadeth out the corn." The law of Moses stated that the ox was allowed to eat grain as it worked. That was its just due. This verse in Deuteronomy is in the context of how God expected the Israelites to treat each other—fairly. Therefore, just as laborers are paid for their work and oxen are paid for theirs, so Paul's physical needs should be met as he ministered spiritually (see also 1 Timothy 5:18). Paul rephrases this principle in verse 11: if he has "sown" unto the Corinthians spiritual things, shouldn't he "reap" from them carnal things? Apparently, the church was supporting others (v. 12), but not Paul. He went on to say that he had not made an issue of it, lest the gospel be hindered.

5. In 1 Corinthians 9:13, Paul gives one more example. What is it?

6. Read Numbers 18:8–24 and share some of the ways the Israelite priests were provided for.

The specifics of what the priests received are listed in William Barclay's commentary on 1 Corinthians.[1] To summarize, with the burnt offering, very little was left, but the priests received the hide to use or sell. With the sin and trespass offerings, only the fat was burned, and the priests received all the flesh. The meat offering consisted of flour, wine, and oil of which the majority went to the priest. With the peace offering, the priest received a portion (the breast and shoulder), the fat and entrails were burned, and the remainder went back to the worshiper. Besides these, the priests received the firstfruits of wheat, barley, the vine, fig tree, pomegranate, olive, and honey.

7. What is Paul's conclusion in 1 Corinthians 9:14 regarding these examples?

[1] William Barclay, *The Letter to the Corinthians*, Daily Study Bible (Philadelphia: The Westminster Press, 1956), 80.

A pastor's wages should be adequate to care for his family's needs. Some pastors are bivocational because their churches have not grown to the point where they can care for their pastors' needs entirely. That is common especially in new churches and in churches in developing countries. But whenever possible, a church should take care of its pastor so that he can dedicate himself to preaching and to the needs of his people.

A Minister's Choices

After teaching this principle, Paul goes on to say in verse 15 that he has not used this right, nor has he written these things so the Corinthian church would begin to support him. He is basically using this as an example of love over liberties or rights. He has every right to receive compensation from each church, but he chooses not to. This was Paul's practice.

8. Read the following verses and explain why Paul many times did not take wages from the churches: Acts 20:33–35; 2 Corinthians 11:8–9; 1 Thessalonians 2:6–9; 2 Thessalonians 3:8.

9. According to Acts 18:1–3, how did Paul support himself in Corinth?

Read 1 Corinthians 9:16–18. Paul had a responsibility, a command if you will, to preach the gospel.

10. (a) Read Acts 9:15–16. After Paul (Saul) was converted, what did the Lord tell Ananias about him?

    (b) What had the Lord told Paul on the road to Damascus, according to Acts 26:13–19?

11. In 1 Corinthians 9:16, Paul talks about the necessity of preaching the gospel—basically that he doesn't have a choice! Read Jeremiah 20:9. What happened to Jeremiah when he tried to keep quiet after God told him to prophesy?

12. In 1 Corinthians 9:17, Paul says "a dispensation of the gospel is committed unto him." Look up *dispensation* in a concordance. What does this phrase mean?

Not only was Paul compelled to preach the gospel, but he chose to preach "without charge" (v. 18). That way he would not be a burden to the churches and no one could accuse him of being in the ministry for the money. So, while Paul had a right to be paid by the churches, he chose not to be.

In 1 Corinthians 9:19–23 Paul moves back to the law of love over liberty. Paul says in verse 19 that he had made himself a servant to all so he might gain the more. In the following verses, he illustrates this principle.

13. (a) According to verse 20, whom did Paul become like?

(b) What do you think he meant by that?

14. (a) Whom does verse 21 say Paul became like?

(b) What do you think this means?

15. When Paul talked about being "like them without the law," what exception did he make?

16. The last example Paul gives is of becoming like the weak. Who were the weak? See 1 Corinthians 8:9–13.

Paul did his best to not offend anyone in his ministry of the gospel so that he could see some come to Christ. His passion was for Christ to be known, so he wouldn't allow his freedoms to hurt that goal. He states four times in 9:19–22 that his goal is that he "might gain" people: the Jews, the Gentiles, the weak—he wanted them all to know Christ.

In verses 24–27, Paul compares the Christian faith to a race. The city of Corinth was familiar with races. The Isthmus Games were one of the main contests and were held right there in Corinth. Contestants ran to win a pine wreath and short-lived acclaim. We believers are also running to obtain a prize, but ours will be incorruptible, eternal.

17. What principle is laid out in verses 25–27 to help Christians run well?

This principle of moderation and self-discipline goes back again to the study on love over law. "I keep under my body" means literally "to buffet or hit under the eye." Paul would knock himself out before he'd allow his desires to take precedence over love. Do you have the self-discipline to abstain from the thing that offends? What is believers' purpose but to glorify God and share His glory with a lost world? Paul would not let his freedoms overshadow the ministry he had been called to do.

18. Read Hebrews 12:1–3. What guidelines are in these verses to help you "run the race"?

Application

As a minister of the gospel, Paul gave his whole being—intellect, emotions, and will—to the work of the ministry. He did not do it for financial reward, and he sacrificed freedoms to be sure he offended no one and could win anyone! Many in full-time ministry today have committed themselves to pouring into the lives of others. For this reason, rather than criticizing or discouraging your pastor, support him and pray for him. Let him know you appreciate him and the time he gives to the Word and to your church's needs. A church should have a loving and respectful relationship between its pastor and people.

Second, be faithful in attendance and service. There is no greater joy to a pastor and his wife than the faithfulness of their church.

Third, be sure your church financially supports your pastor adequately, if possible. It is true that the Lord will meet a pastor's needs, but He has chosen to use the church to do it!

Finally, pray for your pastor! Pray that he will run well, will not grow too weary, will be filled with the Spirit, and will be true to the Word of God. Pray for his family as well, as they sacrifice time with him so he can meet the needs of others.

CHAPTER 9

Learn by Example

1 Corinthians 10:1–13

MANY TIMES WHEN WE THINK of learning by example, we think of someone teaching us the right way to do things. But occasionally, learning by example is learning what not to do! The examples given in 1 Corinthians 10 are all negative, with a warning to the Corinthian believers that the same temptations would come to them.

The chapter begins with "Moreover," which indicates a continuing thought from the previous chapters. Paul had just instructed the Corinthians on the principle of love over liberty. He also illustrated this principle by recounting his life of becoming "all things to all men" in order to minister well. In chapter 10 he warns about the dangers of falling into temptation, as their fathers had done.

What does overcoming temptation have to do with the principle of love over liberty? If we focus on our rights and liberties in Christ, then our focus is not on pleasing Christ and serving others. Those that defend their actions by their liberty in Christ are often living on the very edge of freedom, as close to the line of sin as possible yet in the gray area. Choices become a matter of doing what will make one happy, rather than doing what will make one holy. If you are living this way, with your foot right on the line of a gray area / sin, you are likely to step over that line. Someone who stays clear of that line is much less likely to step over it. Sometimes, in prideful confidence, we assert that we can handle being in close proximity to sin and not give in to it. Paul addresses that dangerous pride near the end of this section.

Paul finishes chapter 9 with his example of self-discipline in order to finish the race well. In 10 he reminds the Corinthian believers of how Israel lacked that discipline, sought to please only themselves, and did not overcome temptation.

Israel's Bad Example in the Wilderness

Read 1 Corinthians 10:1–2.

1. In verse 1, Paul refers to the nation of Israel as "our fathers." Does that mean that all in the Corinthian church were Jewish Christians? See Romans 4:11 and Galatians 3:29.

2. What do the following phrases mean?
   Under the cloud (Exodus 13:21–22)

   Passed through the sea (Exodus 14:15–22)

3. Verse 2 states that the Israelites were all "baptized unto Moses." Read Romans 6:1–10.
   (a) What does baptism today mean?

   (b) How were they "baptized unto Moses"?

Baptism was practiced long before the early church. People who wanted to declare publicly that they followed the teachings of an individual would be baptized by or "to" that individual. Being baptized by John the Baptist, for example, meant that a person identified with his teachings and was his follower. We are baptized today to show that we identify with Christ and His teachings.

4. First Corinthians 10:3–4 says that the Israelites received spiritual meat and spiritual drink. What was Paul referring to here? See Exodus 16:15; 17:6; Nehemiah 9:15, 20; Psalm 78:14–16, 24–25.

5. The word *overthrown* means to "strew" or "spread over."
   (a) With what was God displeased that resulted in forty years of wandering and death in the wilderness? See Numbers 14:29–33.

   (b) What was the Israelites' sin in this instance?

   (c) Can you think of a New Testament verse that corroborates God's displeasure with this sin?

Paul then lists several examples of sins committed by Israel in the wilderness in verses 6–10.

6. List each sin, then give an Old Testament example of the nation of Israel committing this sin, with the reference if possible. In the last column, using a Bible dictionary or concordance, write the definition of that sin.

Sin	Occasion and Reference	Definition of This Sin

7. According to 1 Corinthians 10:6 and 11, why did Paul say these incidents are recorded?

The Seriousness of Sin

This list goes from such serious sins as idolatry and fornication to sins we might consider little, such as lusting and murmuring. Our first response may be, I would never commit idolatry or fornication. We may not bow down to an idol, but many today have made gods of love, success, money, self-image, and the list goes on. Anything that comes before our relationship with the Lord is an idol. Lust, which is an inordinate desire for something, fits with both idolatry and fornication. Lusting for something raises that item to the status of idol; and in the case of fornication, lust is always the precursor. Fornication is becoming more and more common even in Christian circles. Many times it is in the form of visual fornication such as pornography.

What about murmuring? Is that really as serious? Considering that almost fifteen thousand people died for the "little" sin of murmuring, we have to conclude that it is a great offense to God. Though complaining doesn't have the same stigma as fornication in our churches, it is still sin. The self-discipline Paul talked about in chapter 9 includes controlling the tongue!

Each one of these sins displays a lack of trust and contentment in God's direction. In lust, it's "God hasn't given me enough." In idolatry, it's "God is not enough. I want more." Fornication is also a form of idolatry; it is "fulfilling my flesh is more important than honoring God." Tempting ("testing") Christ and murmuring go hand in hand. We are not satisfied with the circumstances of our lives, so we complain, questioning God's goodness and trying His patience.

8. (a) What other verses can you think of that admonish believers for a complaining spirit?

   (b) What is the opposite of a complaining spirit?

9. The word *admonition* in verse 11 includes the concept of instruction and warning. Write this verse in your own words.

10. Read verse 13. In the context of this passage, what do you think temptation means?

11. Read James 1:13–15.
    (a) Is temptation sin?

    (b) What are the steps that lead to death, according to these verses?

12. Read 1 John 2:16.
    (a) What are the three areas of temptation?

    (b) How would you define them?

The lust of the flesh includes any of our fleshly desires: food, sex, and so on. The lust of the eyes is coveting what we see. The pride of life is seeking recognition and advancement (e.g., popularity, power). Every temptation will fall into one of these categories.

13. Identify how each of these three areas is seen in the following verses:

Reference	Lust of the Flesh	Lust of the Eyes	Pride of Life
Genesis 3:6			
Matthew 4:1–10			

One of the most reassuring statements in Scripture is found in the middle of 1 Corinthians 10:13: "God is faithful."

14. What promise is given in verse 13?

We have no excuse for our sin. No believer can claim that "the Devil made me do it" or "I couldn't help it" or "You drove me to it"! God always gives us a way out; He never allows us to be tempted beyond our ability to combat that enticement. We cannot blame our anger on our spouse, our impatience on our children, or our murmuring on our circumstances. As believers, we do not have to sin.

First Corinthians 10:13 is often quoted in the context of suffering—that God will always give a way out of a trial, but that is not true. Based on the Scriptural context, God may not necessarily take us out of difficult circumstances, but He promises that we will be able to handle the difficulty without sinning.

Application

Learn what not to do from these verses in 1 Corinthians 10.

First, don't let your liberty bring you to the edge of sin. In questionable areas, stay as close as you can to the holiness of God. Let your focus be on loving Christ, not self.

Second, take responsibility for your sin. It is no one else's fault. We all sin, but our response to that sin reveals our heart. A heart for God will sorrow over sin and will be quick to repent and confess.

Finally, rejoice in the way out God has given you. In every temptation, remember you do not have to fall. In every trial, ask God to give you strength to respond with a godly attitude without sin. "Now these things were our examples, to the intent we should not. . . ."

LESSON 10

Order in the Church!

1 Corinthians 11

AS WE COME TO CHAPTER 11, Paul closes out the section of love over liberty by encouraging the church to follow his example as he followed Christ. First Corinthians 11:1 should really have been the final verse in chapter 10. Paul then changes direction and seems to be answering other issues that were raised by the church. The two issues addressed in 1 Corinthians 11 are proper decorum in public worship and proper decorum in partaking of the Lord's Supper.

Military personnel know who they are to answer to—who the authority is—because there is a clear chain of command. In corporations, schools, even in the local grocery story, each employee knows who he or she is to answer to. Chaos ensues if no one is in charge. The same is true in the church. God has given us a clear order of command, an order of authority. In the Pastoral Epistles, He gives a specific order for church leadership, but in 1 Corinthians 11, God gives a general order of submission.

Submission, Not Inferiority

Read 1 Corinthians 11:2–16.

1. Give the order of headship listed in verse 3.

2. How do you know that this order of authority does not indicate superiority or inferiority? (Tip: See Luke 22:42.)

3. Submission to authority is not unique to this passage. Who is the head of whom, according to the following passages?
   Ephesians 1:22–23

   Ephesians 5:22

4. What areas of submission to authority are in the following passages?
   Ephesians 5:24

   Ephesians 6:1

   Romans 13:1

Submission, Not Usurpation

First Corinthians 11 seems to indicate that men are to have the authority in the church in general, which is supported by the qualifications for pastor and deacons in 1 Timothy 3. Only men may serve in these positions. First Timothy 2:11–12 also supports this principle, stating that women are not to teach men or usurp authority over them. As women, we should have an attitude of submission, humility, and respect for our church leaders.

5. In verses 5–10, Paul explains how this headship is pictured in the church. What was the sign of submission for the women of the church?

The head covering was a sign of the woman being under authority (v. 10); it was "power on her head." Head coverings in Biblical times were used to signify women's subordinate relationship to men. Today in many Middle Eastern countries, the head covering includes a veil, signifying that the woman's beauty and charms are to be reserved for her husband only.

Just as we see in our day, the Roman Empire also had feminist movements. Feminists in that culture would remove their head coverings and cut their hair to look like men's hair. Marriage and child-rearing were under attack as being unjust to women. If a woman shaved her head, she was either a prostitute or a feminist protesting her role. So Paul was saying that praying without the head covering is the same as shaving the head and is a shameful sign of rebellion. He was reminding the church that God ordained a ruling order so the church can function smoothly. Women were not to usurp a role that was not meant for them to fill, and their submission was indicated by the head covering.

So why do we not cover our heads today? In our Western culture, wearing a covering or hat does not indicate submission or humility. In fact, wearing a hat today might draw attention to ourselves and even be considered ostentatious. The principle of submission in the church today is shown through a humble, submissive attitude to authority. Our headwear or lack thereof has no moral or spiritual significance. However, if someone chooses to wear a head covering, it is certainly acceptable and proper, but that woman should not be judged as more spiritual than the one who does not hold that conviction. The command for women is to dress modestly with humility (1 Timothy 2:9–10), not drawing attention to themselves.

Submission, Not Rebellion

6. In 1 Corinthians 11:7–9 what reason is given for the distinction between men and women?

This passage also brings to light that a woman's hair is given to her as a natural covering. The trend for longer hair on men and butch cuts on women seems to be coming back. But the distinction between men and women is taught throughout Scripture (e.g., Deuteronomy 22:5; 1 Peter 3:7), along with the admonition to embrace those differences. God has made us women unique from men, and that is something to celebrate!

7. Read 1 Corinthians 11:14–15. How does nature itself teach what is appropriate?

There are three stages to hair growth: formation, resting, and fallout. The male hormone testosterone speeds up the stages, whereas the female hormone estrogen slows it down. Few women ever reach the point of baldness, something that is common in men. It is part of the natural process that a woman is able to have longer hair. A woman's hair is referred to as her glory. The Greek word used for long hair can also mean an "ornamental hairdo"; either one distinguishes a woman from a man. The principle here is that whether a woman has short-styled hair or long tresses, she should look like a woman, not a man.

8. In 1 Corinthians 11:11–12, Paul comes back to a precious principle of Scripture despite assigned roles. What is that truth?

Submission and Decorum at the Lord's Table

Paul then turned to the area of proper decorum in partaking of the Lord's Supper. Read 1 Corinthians 11:17–34. The Lord's Supper is one of the ordinances of the New Testament church. An ordinance has symbolic significance and was commanded by Christ. The two ordinances to be practiced by the church are baptism and the Lord's Supper. Baptism symbolizes new life in Christ, picturing our salvation, and identifies us as followers of Christ (Romans 6:3–11). The Lord's Supper, or Communion, is a picture of the death of Christ on the cross. At the Passover meal celebrated with the disciples before the crucifixion, Jesus commanded that His followers practice this ordinance, "in remembrance of me."

According to Acts 2, the early church observed both ordinances on a regular basis. Eventually churches added love feasts, in which they came together to eat, fellowship, and share each other's needs. Letters to and from other churches would be shared, and often money was collected to help widows and orphans. These feasts were often followed by the observance of the Lord's Supper. Notice that Paul uses the words "come together" five times in 1 Corinthians 11.

9. In 1 Corinthians 11:18 and 21, Paul mentions two issues that were occurring in these love feasts. What were they?

Instead of promoting unity in the church, the love feasts were promoting selfishness. In Greek, the word for "divisions" (v. 18) is *schismata,* from which we get our word *schism.* The Corinthians spent their time in argument and self-indulgence. Instead of having "all things common," as in Acts 2:44, the upper class ate greedily, eating what they brought rather than sharing with the poor. The purpose for these feasts had been lost; therefore, Paul said it would be better for the upper class to eat at home (v. 22).

Can you imagine partaking in a feast of bickering and selfishness and then transitioning into the Lord's Supper? The Lord's Supper memorializes the most unselfish act in history, that of the Lord Jesus giving His own life for our redemption. Paul immediately reminded the Corinthian church of the reason for Communion, its seriousness, and its meaning, or what it represents. Paul first reminded them of the institution of the ordinance by Christ as He took of the Passover meal with His disciples. Read Luke 22:13–22.

10. What did the Passover meal memorialize? See Exodus 12:12–14.

11. What do you notice about the cup in Luke 22:17 and 20?

Many American believers are unfamiliar with the traditions of the Passover meal. In his commentary on 1 Corinthians, John MacArthur explains the tradition.[1] Four cups were passed during the meal and were separated by the eating of a symbolic food. First the celebrants would pass a cup, then they would eat bitter herbs dipped in fruit sauce while listening to a message on the meaning of the Passover. Next they would sing a hymn of praise, followed by the second cup. The host would then break the unleavened bread and distribute it. Then they all would eat the main meal, which was a sacrificial lamb. The third cup was passed following the meal, and another hymn of praise (the rest of the Hallel) was sung. Just before leaving, they drank the fourth cup, which celebrated the coming kingdom. The third cup is the one Jesus blessed and which became the cup of communion. He took the cup after supper and said, "This cup is the new testament in my blood, which is shed for you" (Luke 22:20).

12. How did the food eaten in the Passover celebration represent the exodus?

[1] John MacArthur, *1 Corinthians*, The MacArthur New Testament Commentary (Chicago: Moody Bible Institute, 1984), 17:271.

13. At the Passover meal recorded in Luke 22, Jesus said the third cup represented His blood shed for the disciples. Why might He have chosen that cup?

With so much meaning and symbolism in the Lord's Supper, we should never partake of it lightly! Paul gave a stern warning to the Corinthian church as to how Communion should be observed.

14. What warning does Paul give in verses 27–28?

The word *unworthily* is the literal meaning of the Greek word, but it also means "irreverently."

15. How might someone take the Lord's Supper unworthily or irreverently?

The word *damnation* in verse 29 is better translated "judgment." We can never be damned once we are saved, but God does evaluate His children and administer discipline.

16. According to verses 30–32, how did God evaluate and discipline Corinthian believers who partook unworthily?

Paul concludes chapter 11 by stating that these issues needed to be corrected immediately. He would set other matters "in order" when he arrived. This whole chapter basically deals with believers' attitude in worship. Praying ("communicating with God"), prophesying ("communicating God's message to others"), and partaking of the Lord's Supper are all areas of worship. These should be carried out with submission, humility, and reverence.

Application

How can we apply this lesson?

First, as women we have a role in the church, that is, submission to the church's male leadership. That may cause you to bristle inside, but it shouldn't. We find submission to authority in all areas of life; it's a necessity for any functioning organization. To have order in the church, there must be delegated roles. So we should support and respect our leaders with a proper attitude of submission.

Second, we need to keep in mind that submission to authority does not mean inferiority in any way. You may be more intelligent, better spoken, and even more spiritual than some in leadership, and your gifts can be used mightily in the church. Don't use your role as an excuse not to serve.

Finally, be an active participant in the Lord's Supper. "This do in remembrance of me" is a command to all believers, not an option. You need to attend the services in which Communion is observed. When you do partake, do it with a cleansed, focused, and grateful heart.

LESSON 11

Spiritual Gifts Explained

1 Corinthians 12

IN EVANGELICAL CIRCLES TODAY there is much confusion centering on spiritual gifts. What are spiritual gifts? Are they supernatural? Do they exist today? Apparently, the Corinthians were also confused about the role of spiritual gifts in the church. Paul addresses their questions in 1 Corinthians 12—14. This lesson looks at the diversity yet unity of spiritual gifts in 1 Corinthians 12. Lesson 12 addresses the practical use of spiritual gifts in the New Testament church and in the church today.

First we must define a spiritual gift. It is an ability—an equipping for service—entrusted by God to every believer to be used under the control of the Holy Spirit and for God's glory. There are two basic views as to when these gifts are given: (1) they are endowed at salvation, or (2) they are endowed at birth and enhanced or "empowered" at salvation. I hold to the view that we are born with God-given abilities but that at salvation they become enhanced and empowered by the Spirit of God to be used for the furtherance of the gospel. The focus of the gift or talent ceases to be self-centered and becomes centered on the glory of God.

The Origin of Spiritual Gifts

The apostles, and later the church, were given supernatural gifts to verify the gospel message. These miraculous gifts were not given at birth or at salvation, but were given as temporary gifts as the Spirit willed. These "signs and wonders" authenticated the message the apostles were sharing. See Hebrews 2:3–4.

Read 1 Corinthians 12:1–11.

1. In verses 1–3, Paul distinguishes between the power of Satan and the power of the Holy Spirit. How were the Corinthians to ascertain the difference?

In verse 2 Paul refers to their past life as being "carried away" to idols. Before salvation, we are enslaved to sin with the possibility of demonic influence or even possession. We do not lose our freedom when we come to Christ; we find freedom! Paul wanted the Corinthians to understand that not all powers are of God. We need to acknowledge the existence of demons and demonic power. That someone is able to do something miraculous does not mean that person is of God. The key to discernment for the Corinthians was the message being preached, which must be "Jesus is Lord."

2. Reread 1 Corinthians 12:4–6. What three words describe the gifts given to the church?

The words *diversities* and *differences* are the same word in Greek, which means "varieties" or "distinctions." Paul says there are a diversity of gifts, a diversity of administrations, and a diversity of operations. The word *gifts* in verse 4 means "gifts of grace" and refers to the spiritual gifts themselves. The word *administration* in verse 5 means "services" or "ministries." Each gift may lend itself to a variety of ministries. For instance, the gift of teaching may manifest itself in a believer being especially gifted with young children or, at the other end of the age spectrum, in teaching adults. The word *operations* in verse 6 means "effect." It is what is "worked out" or "energized" and is the result of the

Holy Spirit's power. He is the One to make our gifts effective. The outcome of using our spiritual gifts is not up to us and should never discourage us from using our gifts for God's glory. So each of these terms builds on the previous one; we are given spiritual gifts that may be manifested in various ministries, with spiritual results as effected by the Spirit of God.

3. (a) According to verse 7, what Christians are given the "manifestation of the Spirit"?

   (b) Why is the manifestation of the Spirit given?

The Spiritual Gifts

4. As we will discuss in the next lesson, not all gifts were permanent. Paul lists many of the gifts given to the New Testament church in verses 8–10. List the gift and its meaning or how it may have been demonstrated.

Reference	Gift	Meaning
12:8		
12:8		
12:9		
12:9		
12:10		
12:10		
12:10		
12:10		
12:10		

5. Reread verse 11.
   (a) Are believers to seek a certain spiritual gift?

   (b) What is our part in the imparting of the gifts?

6. Read Romans 12:3–8. What gifts mentioned in these verses are not mentioned in 1 Corinthians 12:1–11? Give a brief definition of each one.

Gift	Definition

The Body-Like Nature of Spiritual Gifts

Read 1 Corinthians 12:12–27. Christ's church is to function as a Body, the Body of Christ. Though this Body has many members and a variety of gifts, we are to work together, just as the parts of our physical bodies do. A body depends on its many parts to function properly.

7. Tell how the following parts of our physical bodies depend on each other.
   Brain

Nerves

Heart

Eyes

Hands

Feet

Skeleton

8. (a) According to verse 13, who has been baptized by the Holy Spirit?

   (b) What is Spirit baptism, according to this verse?

The charismatic movement teaches that to be truly spiritual, a Christian must evidence the baptism of the Spirit by speaking in tongues. Nowhere does Scripture present an "evidence" of the baptism of the Spirit. Ephesians 5 and Galatians 5 both give evidences of the filling of the Spirit, but not the baptism. Paul states here that "all" the Corinthians were baptized by one Spirit into one body. With the issues that have been addressed already, we know that many of the Corinthians were carnal, not spiritual, yet there are no exceptions given for Spirit baptism. When we accept Christ, we are baptized by the Spirit into the Body of Christ. Background also doesn't matter: Paul states that whether Jew or Gentile, bond or free, we all become part of one Body.

In the next few verses, Paul stresses the unity of the Body. The Spirit gives the diversity of gifts for the Body to function as a whole. No part of the Body is more or less important than another. In the Corinthian church some gifts were being esteemed as more important than others. Some of the believers were dissatisfied, having deemed their own gifts as unimportant while coveting the showier gifts, such as speaking in tongues. Paul reminded the believers that whether their gift was the "foot" or the "mouth," all gifts were necessary to the function of the Body.

9. According to verse 18, who decides the allocation of gifts?

There seems to have been two sides of this discussion: those who wanted to have no part of the Body without the gift of their choice, and those who were proud of their gift, holding it in higher esteem than other gifts. Paul rebukes the first group in verses 15–17 and the second group in verses 21–24.

10. (a) In verses 22–24, how does Paul compare the type of gift with our bodies?

    (b) What are some examples of the "less comely" but necessary parts of the human body?

11. (a) How would you relate this analogy to the body to the church today?

    (b) What might be some gifts that are not comely or noticeable?

12. Paul is emphasizing unity throughout this entire passage. One aspect of unity is seen in verse 26. What is it?

What happens when you stub your toe? What if you have a headache? When one part of the physical body hurts, your whole body is affected. That is how the Body of Christ is to be. We are one, and we respond as one with joy or sorrow.

Read verses 28–31. Paul lists the gifts that God has set in order in the Body. In coveting the miraculous gifts, the Corinthians were devaluing the gifts that God held as most important.

13. What are the first three gifts?

The other gifts mentioned are miracles, healings, helps, governments, and tongues. The gift of helps (v. 28) would be the same one mentioned in Romans 12 as "ministering." It means taking the burden off someone and placing it on oneself. What a precious gift to any spiritual leader!

"Governments" (v. 28) is the gift of leadership. It literally means "to steer or pilot a ship." Can all be apostles or pastors? Not everyone can be the pilot. God does not intend for all believers to have gifts that are "up front" and noticed. The Body needs many unseen members to carry on the work. Paul lists the gift of tongues last—the gift the Corinthians were coveting—and challenges them to desire the higher gifts instead. As he closes the chapter, he segues into chapter 13, desiring unity and love above all.

14. Take a few minutes to consider what your spiritual gift(s) may be. Write down any that you believe are possibilities.

Application

Do you know how God has gifted you? What should you do if you are unsure? First, think about what you enjoy in serving the Lord. If you have a natural love in an area of service, that may be where God has gifted you. Second, ask someone close to you what he or she thinks your spiritual gifts are.

Finally, as you use your gifts to edify the Body of Christ, do not overestimate or underestimate your importance to the Body. Every part of the body is important, whether it is a shoulder to cry on or a big toe to give balance to the whole. We also need to remember that the gifts come from the Holy Spirit; we have no room to boast in how we serve.

The unity of the Body is so important. Never let what you are asked to do or not asked to do become a reason for disunity. "Whether therefore ye eat, or drink, or whatsoever ye do, do all to the glory of God" (1 Corinthians 10:31).

LESSON 12

Spiritual Gifts Applied

1 Corinthians 13; 14

IN THE MIDDLE OF PAUL'S EXPLANATION of spiritual gifts in chapters 12—14, we find the "Love Chapter," 1 Corinthians 13. It is heard at most weddings and espoused often for describing "true love"—as it should be! But we often forget the context of the passage; not only does love trump liberty, but love also trumps spiritual gifts! In the middle of this dissertation on gifts, Paul reminded the Corinthian church that all their gifts were worth nothing if love was not presiding over them. While the Corinthians were coveting and arguing over certain spiritual gifts, they were causing disunity in the Body. They were leaving out the fact that any gift used for the Body of Christ must be bathed in love. The Greek word for love in this passage is *agape,* a love demonstrated by God in the unselfish and merciful gift of His Son. Agape is totally unconditional love focused on the object of that love. Agape is to be demonstrated not only in a marriage relationship, but also in the Body of Christ.

Love Trumps Spiritual Gifts

Read 1 Corinthians 13.

1. Paul names several spiritual gifts in verses 1–3. What are they?

A "sounding brass" is a noisy gong. Paul says that speaking in tongues ("languages") sounds like a gong or a clanging cymbal if it is done with no evidence of love. Clearly, the gift of tongues was not to be used out of pride or selfish motives, but for ministering to others in love. Since the rites honoring the pagan deities included speaking in strange noises accompanied by gongs, cymbals, and trumpets, Paul was comparing the gift of tongues without love to that pagan ritual.

Along with tongues, what good are prophecy, wisdom, knowledge, and faith if they are not exercised in love for the edifying of the Body of Christ? Here Paul addresses the motives behind the spiritual gifts. Each of these gifts is not to be used in pride for self-glory, but for the good of others. Even the gift of giving can be expressed without love. So Paul says that if you give "all [your] goods to feed the poor" but not in love, there is no profit for you. Notice Paul doesn't say it doesn't profit the one you're giving to, but that there is no eternal reward, no spiritual growth or blessing in giving, if the motive is not love.

2. (a) What other motives for giving might people have?

   (b) Can you think of a Biblical example of giving with the wrong motive?

As you read through the description of love in chapter 13, understanding the context of spiritual gifts and the Body of Christ, love takes on a whole new dimension!

3. List the characteristics of love in 1 Corinthians 13:4–7 with a brief explanation of what these characteristics mean. Notice that love is described not by feelings but by actions.

Verse	What Love Does	What That Means
13:4		
13:4		
13:4		
13:4		
13:5		
13:5		
13:5		
13:5		
13:6		
13:7		
13:7		
13:7		
13:7		

Paul was reminding the Corinthian church that just as love trumps liberty, love also trumps any gift. Love doesn't vaunt itself or boast of a gift, and love exercises her gift for the good of the church members, not for self-glorification. Love also rejoices in others' gifts and does not envy them. Each of these characteristics of love can be applied to the way we use our gifts in the Body. The way a person treats another member of the Body is far more important than the gifts that person exercises. No matter how well we serve, if we don't demonstrate love for others, our service is empty.

In verses 8–10 we see the cessation of the gifts. Verse 8 uses three words for the finality of the gifts: "fail," "cease," and "vanish away." The words *fail* and *vanish away* are from the same Greek word meaning "to render inoperative," "to abolish." It is a passive form of the verb, meaning that something or someone else will cause them to stop. The word *cease* has the meaning of "to stop, to come to an end." The verb tense indicates that the thing—in this case, tongues—is self-limiting; it will stop by itself.

4. Verse 9 implies one of the reasons for these gifts that will fail, cease, and vanish away.
   (a) What is that reason?

   (b) How does that relate to the spiritual gifts?

Verse 10 goes on to say that the sign gifts would cease "when that which is perfect is come." What is that perfect thing that will cause the sign gifts to cease? Some take the view that this is referring to the second coming of Christ, but the sign gifts had already ceased—for hundreds of years. The word *that* is a gender neutral word probably referring to a thing rather than a person. It would seem rather that this statement refers to the completion of the perfect Word of God, which contains all that we need to know God and walk with Him (2 Peter 1:3). Revelation would no longer be needed, since the complete revelation of God would be available.

5. According to Hebrews 2:3–4, why were these sign gifts given?

All the sign gifts were either to (1) communicate the word from God (gifts: wisdom, knowledge, interpretation of tongues, prophecy, faith, discerning of spirits) or to (2) authenticate the message being given (gifts: healings, miracles, tongues). Neither purpose is necessary now that the canon of Scripture is complete.

Read 1 Corinthians 13:11–13. Paul here compares the partial gifts to a child gaining knowledge. "I spake as a child" (tongues), "I understood as a child" (knowledge), and "I thought as a child" (wisdom and prophecy). Paul knew that as the Word of God would be revealed, the church would become more mature and discerning. The supernatural gifts were, therefore, needed only in infancy, when there was limited revelation. Paul suggested that the baby church could see only in a blurry mirror. Conversely, the reflection of the mirror of the Word of God reveals to us what is lacking.

6. What does James 1:22–25 say should be our response to the "perfect law of liberty"?

Paul concludes chapter 13 with a summary of what is important. After all the supernatural gifts have ceased, faith, hope, and love will remain; and the most important is love.

Right Use of Spiritual Gifts Doesn't Lead to Confusion

In chapter 14, Paul gives practical instructions in the use of the miraculous gifts. Not only were the Corinthians coveting the wrong gifts, but they were also exercising their gifts in a way that caused confusion.

7. Read 1 Corinthians 14:1–6. Paul is comparing two gifts, prophesying and speaking in tongues.
   (a) Which does Paul say is better?

   (b) Why?

8. In verses 7–12, Paul compares tongues to instruments without clear sounds or a trumpet with "an uncertain sound." Summarize what he is saying.

9. Read verses 13–20. Why does Paul say that speaking in tongues without an interpreter is unfruitful?

The gift of speaking in tongues, so coveted by the Corinthian church, was basically a pointless gift if there was no interpreter. In verse 19 Paul stresses that saying five words with understanding is much more profitable than speaking ten thousand words in an unknown tongue.

10. According to verses 21–24, what was the purpose of tongues and of prophesying?

11. (a) According to Paul, if unbelievers came into the church and observed everyone speaking in tongues, how would they respond?

    (b) What if they observed prophesying instead?

12. Read Ephesians 4:11–16. What is the purpose for the gifts and of the local church?

Today many churches have moved away from the purpose of the local church as given in Ephesians and have become "seeker sensitive." No Scripture supports the concept that the local church is where unbelievers come to be saved. The purpose of the local church is to train believers in the Word of God so that they may go out and win the lost. Unbelievers may visit and hopefully hear the gospel, but the church is a body of and for believers. Let's not lose our purpose!

First Corinthians 13 teaches us that the miraculous sign gifts would cease. The sign gifts did cease—for over fifteen hundred years. There is no mention of speaking in tongues, other than in demonic séances, from the time of Scripture until 1901. We do not believe the present-day use of signs, as seen in the charismatic/Pentecostal movement, are of the Holy Spirit. Scripture teaches that the signs would cease, and they did. With the Scriptures completed, there would be no purpose for the signs.

The remainder of 1 Corinthians 14 is dedicated to guidelines for the use of gifts in the church. Another reason we know that the present-day signs are not of God is that they do not follow the Biblical procedures given in chapter 14.

Read 1 Corinthians 14:26–40, where Paul admonishes all the Corinthians for trying to participate in the sign gifts. They were not interested in edifying or learning, but only in self-glorification and attention.

13. What "rules" in verses 27–28 did Paul give for speaking in tongues?

14. What about prophesying in verses 29–32?

Prophesying could either be reiterating what had already been taught by the apostles or giving new revelation. Those with the gift of discernment would be able to judge the validity of the prophetic messages. When verse 32 states that the "spirits of the prophets are subject to the prophets," it means that the prophets' spiritual activities were under the prophets' full control. No one could say they had no control over what they said;

the prophets would be fully aware of all they were prophesying, though they may not have understood it completely.

15. In 1 Corinthians 14:34–35 what is the command regarding women?

This is one of the commands being ignored in present-day speaking in tongues. Women are often the primary contributors, disobeying this clear command. If this sign were truly of God, it would be subject to His Word.

Paul encouraged the believers to apply these commandments from the Lord to their practice of the spiritual gifts. He reminded them to give proper importance to prophecy and to regulate the use of tongues.

16. In verses 33 and 40, with what statement does Paul conclude this section on the gifts?

Application

Though chapters 12—14 are on spiritual gifts, Paul emphasized two important virtues: unity and love. When our gifts are not exercised in love or they cause disunity, they do more harm than good. As you use your gift in the Body of Christ, be sure you use it in love, for the edifying of the Body.

The doctrine regarding the cessation of the sign gifts is important. The charismatic movement has caused confusion throughout the evangelical world. For further reading, see *Charismatic Confusion* by Ernest Pickering and Myron Houghton and *Speaking in Tongues and Divine Healing* by Robert Lightner.

We should rejoice in whatever way the Lord has gifted us to serve Him. Recognize your part in the Body of Christ and the fact that each member is just as important as any other member. If each one of us would strive to be the best she can be as a hand, a foot, an eye, the brain, or the nerves of the body, we can work together to accomplish so much for God's glory. As we use whatever gift we have been blessed with to serve Christ and His Body, the church will become a well-functioning, loving unit. You are needed. You are important. Now use your gift!

CHAPTER 13

The Resurrection, Our Hope

1 Corinthians 15; 16

FOR A BELIEVER IN CHRIST, the resurrection is the kingpin of our doctrine. Romans 10:9 says, "That if thou shalt confess with thy mouth the Lord Jesus, and shalt believe in thine heart that God hath raised him from the dead, thou shalt be saved." Without the resurrection there is no salvation. Without the resurrection there is no reason to give our lives for the gospel. But, because the resurrection of Jesus Christ guarantees our future resurrection, we can serve with joy!

It is hard to fathom how someone who does not believe in an afterlife can go on day after day. On one hand, such a person would do everything he or she could to delay death, because that would end that person's existence. On the other hand, thinking that this life is all there is would be very disheartening. Paul refers to it as being miserable.

Paul states the issue facing the Corinthian church in 1 Corinthians 15:12. Simply put, some were saying that there is no resurrection of the dead. They were not denying Christ's resurrection per se, but they did not transfer the truth of His resurrection to the believer's bodily resurrection when Christ comes again. Many may have believed in the immortality of the soul but not in the resurrection of the body. It is to our benefit that this was an issue, because it resulted in one of the greatest chapters in the Word of God on the theme of the resurrection.

The Gospel Requires the Resurrection

Read 1 Corinthians 15:1–11.

1. A definition of the gospel is given in verses 1–4. How would you summarize it?

Verses 5–8 name the ones to whom Christ appeared after His resurrection. Two or three witnesses were all that were required for proof in a court of law, yet here were over five hundred witnesses to the resurrection of Christ, most still alive at the time of this letter.

2. Paul talks about Christ's appearance to the apostles and then Christ's appearance to him "as of one born out of due time" ("untimely born"). What did Paul mean by this statement?

Paul's conversion on the road to Damascus (Acts 9) was unlike any other apostle's experience. Yet he was a "chosen vessel" (v. 15), and by God's grace he became a writer of Scripture. What an encouragement to those whose upbringing was less than ideal, who are trapped in sin, who don't even believe in God. God can take a willing heart from any background, transform a person for His glory, and use that person in a remarkable way. Paul is an example of the power of the grace of God.

Life without a Resurrected Christ Is Depressing

3. Read 1 Corinthians 15:12–19. These verses give the depressing picture of life without a resurrected Christ. List the consequences described in these verses if there is no resurrection.

One of the most triumphant statements in Scripture is found in verse 20: "But now is Christ risen from the dead"! More than five hundred brethren could affirm that Christ had risen bodily from the grave. Christ's resurrection was "the firstfruits" of those who have died.

4. Read Leviticus 23:10 and Romans 11:16.
   (a) What were firstfruits?

   (b) How is Christ the "firstfruits of them that slept"?

Christ Brought Resurrection

Read 1 Corinthians 15:21–34. Paul contrasts what Adam brought with what Christ brought. By Adam came death; by Christ comes the resurrection from the dead, that is, life. Verses 22–24 give the order of the resurrection.

5. In verse 23, who does Paul say will raise second, that is, after Christ, the firstfruit? (See also 1 Thessalonians 4:15–17.)

6. (a) What will happen at "the end" (v. 24)?

   (b) What does this refer to?

In His millennial reign, Christ will have all authority and power, and all creation will be subject to Him. Verse 26 says that the last enemy to be destroyed is death. So, at the conclusion of the Millennium, the final resurrection will take place, and all unbelieving dead will be raised to face the Great White

Throne Judgment. Death will be no more. The eternal state of joy in Heaven or torment in Hell will begin. Death will have been conquered.

What Does "Baptized for the Dead" Mean?

First Corinthians 15:29 is a difficult verse to interpret and has become the basis for errant doctrine. When interpreting any verse in Scripture, we must be careful not to interpret it without considering the rest of Scripture. Verse 29 says, "Else what shall they do which are baptized for the dead . . . ? Why are they then baptized for the dead?" Based on our knowledge of other Scriptures, we know that this does not mean that one person can be baptized for someone already dead to guarantee that person's salvation. First of all, baptism is not part of salvation (Ephesians 2:8–9); rather, it is an identification to the world that someone is a follower of Christ. No dead person can be helped by another person's baptism. "It is appointed unto men once to die, but after this the judgment" (Hebrews 9:27).

So what might Paul have meant? Here is one possible explanation in light of the context, including the verses following verse 29.

In the New Testament church, those who professed Christ as Savior were usually baptized immediately. Being saved was not synonymous with being baptized, but one assumed the other. So "they . . . which are baptized" may simply refer to those who had been saved and were professing followers of Jesus.

The Greek word *huper,* translated "for" in verse 29, can be translated into more than a dozen other words in the English language, including "because of." Therefore, this phrase could be translated, "What shall they do who have been saved because of [or due to] the testimony of the dead?" Paul may simply have been saying that those who were being saved due to the testimony of those who had died were being saved in vain. If those who had gone on before, leaving a testimony to others, were never going to rise again, why should anyone follow in their faith? In light of verse 30 and following, Paul may have been referring to the amazing testimony of the Christians who had been martyred, whose testimony led to the salvation of many others.

Believers during this time faced persecution daily, many losing their lives. If Christ did not rise, why would they hazard their very lives to preach to others a false hope?

Resurrection Makes a Difference

Hebrews 11, referred to as the "Faith Chapter," tells us of many who gave their lives for their faith in Christ.

7. Read Hebrews 11:32–35. What reason is given for faithfulness even unto death?

Without the resurrection, passion for serving the Lord is foolish. Not only would we have no motivation for service, we would also have no motivation for sanctification.

8. According to the last part of 1 Corinthians 15:32, what would be a fitting motto without the resurrection?

If there is no resurrection, there is no judgment, no accountability. So live for the present! However, looking forward to the resurrection will result in our sanctification.

9. Look up 1 John 3:1–3. What causes a child of God to purify her- or himself?

Paul contradicts the "for tomorrow we die" philosophy in 1 Corinthians 15:33–34. In verse 33, Paul warns the Corinthians not to be deceived. He reminds them that bad company corrupts good morals. They were listening to those who had no knowledge of God and buying into their philosophy. The theology of no resurrection will result in a lifestyle of selfish living. The words "Awake to righteousness, and sin not" in verse 34 literally mean "Come to your right mind and stop sinning!"

What Will Believers' Resurrected Bodies Be Like?

Read 1 Corinthians 15:35–50. The next question Paul addresses is What will the resurrected body be like? Paul makes several comparisons and contrasts in these verses.

10. The first comparison is given in verses 36–37. How does sowing a seed compare to the resurrection of a body? See also John 12:24.

Verses 39–41 list many of the different "bodies" created by God. Each "flesh" is unique with varying glories. Even as we have the "flesh of men," our resurrected bodies will also be of that "flesh," only better! The differences are described in verses 42–44.

11. (a) What differences between the body sown ("dying") and the body raised are mentioned in verses 42–44?

    (b) Summarize how our glorified bodies will be different.

The older I get, the more I look forward to a new body, free from sickness, aging, pain, and sin. What would we have to look forward to without the hope of the resurrection?

Another comparison is then given of what Paul calls the first Adam and the second Adam (Christ). Just as we were created of the earth with flesh and blood like the first Adam, so will we also bear the image of the second Adam in incorruption, as heavenly beings.

What If We Don't Die?

Read 1 Corinthians 15:51–58. Some of the Corinthians must have wondered, What if we live until Christ returns? Will we never receive a new body? Paul then describes the mystery of the church in the Rapture, a truth not revealed in the Old Testament Scriptures.

12. Describe the order of events listed in verses 51–52 as well as in 1 Thessalonians 4:15–17, which describe the Rapture.

13. What happens "in a moment, in the twinkling of an eye"?

The word *moment* in verse 52 is the Greek word *atomai,* which means "that which cannot be divided." We get our word *atom* from this Greek word, because scientists thought it was the smallest particle of matter and could not be divided. (Of course, we have since split the atom.) The smallest fraction of time, a time that cannot be divided, is the speed at which we will receive our new bodies. "In the twinkling of an eye" refers to the quick movement or gleam in the eye, which is almost imperceptible. This change will basically be instantaneous. Notice that this word is used to describe the glorification of our bodies, not our ascent to the clouds. Nowhere does Scripture say we will simply disappear or even ascend rapidly. The gathering together of the believers into the clouds may possibly be visible to all. The disciples watched as Christ ascended to Heaven. If we ascend in a similar way, the whole world may be watching!

Our bodies will then have put on incorruption (no longer subject to decay or deterioration) and immortality (no longer subject to death). The resurrection means victory over death!

14. How does verse 58 tie in with the thoughts of the resurrection?

The doctrine of the resurrection changes everything! It is the basis of our salvation, service, and sanctification. Our labor is not in vain in the Lord!

Paul Concludes

Paul concluded his letter to the church at Corinth with some final practical instructions and greetings. Another whole lesson could be written on the instructions and individuals mentioned, but we will just hit some key thoughts.

15. Read 1 Corinthians 16:1–2.
    (a) When were the Corinthians to gather their offerings?

    (b) What was to be the basis of how much they gave?

Paul promised to visit them soon and maybe even spend the winter with them. He also updated them regarding the plans of Timothy (v. 10) and Apollos (v. 12).

16. What are some of Paul's final words of advice to the church, found in 16:13–14? (Tip: Look for five admonitions.)

17. Paul mentions three men who ministered to him and refreshed him. What are their names?

Paul also mentions Aquila and Priscilla, a couple he met in Corinth (Acts 18:1–2). They were in Ephesus, hosting a house church, when Paul wrote this letter. He sent their greetings and closed with his own blessing on the church.

Application

How should the resurrection affect you? First of all, rejoice! This life is not all there is! Second, serve God with all your heart. It will be worth it all when we see Jesus! Finally, allow Him to conform you to His image so that you will not be ashamed at His coming.

I love that 1 Corinthians closes with the great encouragement of the resurrection. The hope of the resurrection makes all our sacrifices in this life worth them all. "Therefore, my beloved brethren, be ye stedfast, unmoveable, always abounding in the work of the Lord, forasmuch as ye know that your labour is not in vain in the Lord" (1 Corinthians 15:58).

Conclusion

First Corinthians is a book full of doctrinal and practical issues, with much to challenge us and guide us to a mature walk with Christ. I pray that you have grown in your knowledge of the Word through this study, understanding the Biblical answers to today's issues, resulting in a closer walk with Christ and a desire to please Him in all you do.

Leader's Guide

Suggestions for Leaders

The effectiveness of a group Bible study usually depends on the leader and the women's commitment to prepare beforehand and interact during the study. You cannot totally control the second factor, but you have total control over the first one. These brief suggestions will help you be an effective Bible study leader.

Prepare each lesson a week in advance. During the week, read supplemental material and look for illustrations in the everyday events of your life and in the lives of others.

Encourage the women to complete each lesson before the meeting itself. This preparation will make the discussion more interesting.

The physical setting in which you meet will have some bearing on the study itself. Choose an informal setting that will encourage women to relax and participate. In addition, create an atmosphere in which women feel free to participate and be themselves.

During the discussion time, here are a few things to observe.

- Don't do all the talking; this study is not a lecture.
- Encourage discussion of each question by adding ideas and questions.
- Don't discuss controversial issues that will divide the group. (Differences of opinion are healthy; divisions are not.)
- Don't allow one woman to dominate the discussion. Draw others into the study by saying, "Let's hear from someone on this side of the room" (the side opposite the dominant talker) or "Let's hear from someone who has not shared yet today."
- Stay on the subject. One of your responsibilities as the leader is to keep the group on track.
- Don't get bogged down on a question that interests only one person.
- When there is no right or wrong answer to a question, the answer key says "answers may vary." Other questions are personal, so the key says "personal answers." In either case, this doesn't mean the question cannot be answered aloud, just that the question will be answered from a personal perspective. If you invite women to respond aloud, keep in mind the points listed above to keep your discussion uplifting and on track. You may want to use the last fifteen minutes of the scheduled time for prayer. If you have a large group of learners, divide into smaller groups for prayer.

If you have a morning Bible study, encourage the women to go out for lunch with someone else from time to time. This is a good way to get acquainted. Occasionally you could plan a time when the women bring their own lunches or salads to share and eat together. These things help promote fellowship and friendship in the group.

The formats that follow are suggestions only and can be adapted for your needs.

2-hour Bible Study

10:00—10:15	Coffee and fellowship time
10:15—10:30	Get-acquainted time *Have two women take five minutes each to tell something about themselves and their families.* *Also use this time to make announcements and, if appropriate, take an offering for the babysitters.*
10:30—11:45	Bible study *Leader guides discussion of the questions in the day's lesson.*
11:45—12:00	Prayer time

2-hour Bible Study

10:00—10:45	Bible lesson *Leader teaches a lesson on the content of the material. No discussion during this time.*
10:45—11:00	Coffee and fellowship
11:00—11:45	Discussion time *Divide into small groups with an appointed leader for each group. Discuss the questions in the day's lesson.*
11:45—12:00	Prayer time

1½-hour Bible Study

10:00—10:30	Bible study *Leader guides discussion of half the questions in the day's lesson.*
10:30—10:45	Coffee and fellowship
10:45—11:15	Bible study *Leader continues discussion of the questions in the day's lesson.*
11:15—11:30	Prayer time

Answers

A Personal Note to Study Leaders

This study is designed to be a meaty study of 1 Corinthians. It contains thirteen lessons so it can be used in Sunday School or as a women's Bible study. Answers to all the questions are below, sometimes with additional helpful information. I would suggest you complete the lesson on your own and then use the answers to add to your teaching.

Whether you are an experienced Bible study leader or brand new, I believe you will find enough background and doctrinal information to be able to teach this without a lot of additional study. I love digging into the Word and have attempted to do that for you. I hope you learn as much as I did!

LESSON 1

1. The chief ruler of the synagogue mentioned in Acts 18.
2. Those sanctified ("set apart from sin unto God") in Christ Jesus, those "called to be saints."
3. All those who have called on Jesus' name—anywhere.
4. (a) Answers may vary. (*Saint* comes from the Greek word *hagios,* meaning "sacred" or "holy"; "blameless" and "pure.") (b) Blameless and holy in love. (c) Believers are both chosen and called to be holy.
5. Conformed to the image of God's Son.
6. Positional—"Behold, what manner of love the Father hath bestowed upon us, that we should be called the sons [children] of God" (v. 1). Progressive—"And every man that hath this hope in him purifieth himself" (v. 3). Perfect—"When he shall appear, we shall be like him" (v. 2).
7. (a) They had been enriched by God and lacked no spiritual gift. (Paul specifically mentions utterance ["discourse," "reasoning"] and knowledge.) (b) "Grace of God which is given you by Jesus Christ"; "enriched by him."
8. Believers will be confirmed ("guaranteed") until the end and be found blameless in Christ. (Our salvation and sanctification are secure!)
9. Possible answers: John 10:28–30; Ephesians 1:13–14; 4:30; 1 John 3:19–20.
10. Divisions and contentions.
11. To speak the same thing so there were no divisions and to be joined together in the same mind and judgment ("opinion," "understanding").
12. By doing nothing through strife or vainglory ("rivalry," "conceit"); by being humble ("lowliness of mind"); by counting others as more significant than themselves; by looking to the interests of others, that is, not being self-consumed; and by having the mind of Christ (servanthood).
13. Following a man rather than the Word. The Corinthians were dividing based on their favorite personality.
14. One plants the seed of the gospel and another waters it. (We may have the opportunity to share the gospel; someone else may follow up on that first witnessing opportunity; and another may actually lead the person to Christ.)

15. (a) Someone may have an effect on a life just by her testimony. That may be the planting, while someone else may water that seed by sharing the gospel. It may take several different encounters with Christians for someone to come to Christ. (b) Personal testimonies. (c) God is the One Who gives the increase. Each witness is simply a minister of God. Paul mentions twice that it is God Who gives the increase.
16. Paul separates the gospel from baptism, affirming that Christ sent him to preach the gospel, not to baptize. If baptism were part of salvation, Paul's ministry would have included both.
17. Husbandry ("field") and building.
18. Carnal ("fleshly") and babes (rather than spiritual adults).
19. Rom. 16:7—to mark ("look at," "behold," "watch," "contemplate") and avoid them; 2 Thess. 3:6, 14—to note the person, withdraw from him, and have no company with him so he may be ashamed. God takes very seriously those who cause division in Christ's Body.

LESSON 2

1. (a) The preaching of the cross. (b) Personal answers.
2. Isa. 29:10–14—prophets, rulers, and seers (those who "predict events or developments," those "credited with extraordinary moral and spiritual insight"); Matt. 15:1–9—scribes and Pharisees. (Paul may have been referring to the philosophical leaders of the day, including the debaters, that is, Greeks trained in rhetoric, and the religious leaders such as scribes, the Jewish scholars who handled details of the Mosaic law.)
3. (a) The Jews were looking for a political Savior, not a personal one. They wanted a sign from Heaven. But no sign was good enough for them—not even Jesus' resurrection from the dead. Jesus was an offense, a criminal. Also, the Mosaic law was all important to them, but Jesus emphasized mercy over the law. (b) The Greeks, who prized learning and philosophy, would consider a common man, crucified on a cross, of no account. They were looking for something that made sense. They were rationalists, and God becoming man to die on a cross was not rational to them. (c) Personal answers.
4. (a) Christ becomes the power of God. Through Christ's power, we are saved (Rom. 1:16). And He becomes the wisdom of God. (Christ is wisdom. Wisdom begins with the fear of the Lord. See Proverbs 1 and 8.) (b) Personal answers.
5. Chosen—things that are foolish, weak, base, despised, and "not," or worthless. Not chosen—many wise, mighty, or noble.
6. So that no human will glory and all the glory will go to God.
7. (a) Not with excellency of speech or wisdom; in weakness, fear, and trembling; not with enticing speech; focused on "Jesus Christ, and him crucified." (b) The Spirit and His power.
8. Exod. 4:2—a rod; Num. 22:32–33—a donkey; Josh. 2:1–15—Rahab, a prostitute; Judg. 4:21—Jael, a woman with a nail; Judg. 6:11–15—Gideon, the least in his house; Judg. 7:19–21—only three hundred men versus multitudes; also lamps, pitchers, and trumpets; others—personal answers.
9. (a) They crucified Christ. (b) It was hidden, a mystery.
10. The mystery of the gospel. (Jesus' death, burial, and resurrection to redeem

["buy back"] mankind was not understood by the Jewish nation. It was a mystery revealed in Jesus Christ to the believers.)

11. (a) By the Holy Spirit. (b) Personal answers.
12. *Illumination* means "spiritual enlightenment," "to brighten with light," "clarify, elucidate."
13. A person who has the Holy Spirit has spiritual discernment. That person is able to understand spiritual truths, but the unsaved person does not even "ascertain" or understand believers.
14. Personal answers.

LESSON 3

1. (a) Work. (b) Whatever good things we do for the Lord.
2. (a) Gold, silver, precious stones, wood, hay, and stubble. (b) Fire. (The value of our works lies in whether they are flammable and burn up. Note that flammability increases as the list progresses.)
3. Gold, silver, and precious stones—constructive, helping the church and the cause of Christ; wood, hay, and stubble—worthless; they have no value for eternity.
4. The kingdom of God and His righteousness.
5. 1 Cor. 9:24–25—an incorruptible crown for those who run well; 2 Tim. 4:8—a crown of righteousness for all those who love Christ's appearing; James 1:12; Rev. 2:10—the "crown of life" for those who remain faithful even through tribulation; 1 Pet. 5:1–4—a "crown of glory" for faithful pastors.
6. Lay them at Jesus' feet!
7. By attributing their service to their own wisdom or abilities. (All the glory belongs to God. When we forget that, we are serving with the wrong motive.)
8. Faithfulness. (You might want to mention Joseph and other faithful stewards mentioned in the Bible. Genesis 39:4–6 and 8–9 gives the account of Joseph as a steward in Potiphar's house, entrusted with his master's house and possessions.)
9. (a) Individual responses. (A dictionary definition of *faithfulness* is "strict or thorough in the performance of a duty"; "true to one's word, promises, etc."; "steady in allegiance or affection, loyal, constant"; and "reliable, trusted, believed.") (b) Personal answers.
10. (a) The "counsels ["purposes"] of the hearts." (b) Every believer will receive commendation from the Father—if the purposes of that believer's heart were pure.
11. Arrogance. (The Corinthian believers were proud of who they were and what they possessed. They were attributing their accomplishments to their own abilities.)
12. He reminds them that everything they are and have comes from God. They have no reason to glory in it. They need to give God the glory for any service they are able to accomplish. (Our motivation for service should be the glory of God.)
13. (a) A spectacle to the world, angels, and men. (b) The word *spectacle* means "theater," referring either to the gladiator contests or to a triumphal procession of a Roman general bringing captured soldiers to the arena. (These would be sentenced to death and were paraded before the mocking crowds.

Paul goes on to explain how they had been treated by the world and were viewed as "the filth of the world.")

14. Hunger, thirst, nakedness, buffeting ("beating"), homelessness, hard work, reviling, persecution, defamation.
15. Imprisonment, beatings, whippings, stoning, shipwreck, and trying to survive in the water. He faced dangers from rivers, robbers, false brethren, the Jews, and the Gentiles. He faced dangers in the city, the wilderness, and the sea and from hunger, thirst, cold, and exposure. Plus he had the stress of caring for the churches.
16. Timothy.

LESSON 4

1. Fornication. A man was having relations with his stepmother. That it is called "fornication," not "adultery," probably means the father had died or that he and his wife had divorced. ("Should have" [KJV] is "has" in the ESV. The Greek word is in the present tense, indicating that the fornication had been going on for some time and was still going on.)
2. (a) This kind of fornication violated the Mosaic law and was considered incest. It was the same as relations between him and his own mother. (b) The guilty parties were to be put to death.
3. Rather than mourning, they were arrogant about it. (Paul addresses their pride and arrogance over and over again. Somehow they had rationalized this wicked behavior instead of confronting it.)
4. He needed to be delivered "unto Satan for the destruction of the flesh."
5. Personal answers. (It means to be taken out of the protection and fellowship of the church. The church would be committing the man to "Satan's domain," the world.)
6. It would result in the "destruction of the flesh." (The literal meaning is "ruin of his body." This could mean physical discipline from the Lord [sickness or death] or the natural consequences of fornication.)
7. Leaven. (As leaven permeates a loaf of bread, so evil can permeate a church.)
8. (a) No one was to "keep company" with such Christians, not even to eat with them. (b) Personal answers. (This means no socializing with someone under discipline.)
9. Paul differentiates between one who is "called a brother" and one who is "of this world." (This command says to not associate with someone who professes to be a Christian but is living in sin.) Step 1: The offended person needs to go to the brother or sister and confront the sin. Step 2: If the offender doesn't repent / make it right, then two or three witnesses should be taken for a second confrontation. Step 3: If the offender still doesn't repent and make it right, then the matter is taken to the church. Step 4: If the offender will not listen to the church, he or she is to be treated as a heathen, which necessitates removal from church membership. (The practical application in 1 Corinthians would then be in effect.)
10. There seemed to be true repentance and turning from sin. His letter resulted in carefulness, clearing of themselves, indignation (toward sin), and zeal. (True repentance results in a change of behavior.)
11. To judge those that are within it.

12. Christians taking each other to court.
13. It would seem that Christ's followers will be judging during the Millennium. Matthew refers to the positions given to the apostles, but 1 Corinthians 6:2–3 indicates that all saints will be part of the judicial system, even over the angels. (There are angels "in everlasting chains under darkness unto the judgment of the great day" [Jude 1:6].)
14. Deal with the matter within the church. Find a believer who could help discern and judge the matter. Or take the wrong, allowing yourself to be defrauded rather than taking the believer to court before unbelievers.

LESSON 5

1.

Word	Refers to
Fornicators	Primarily those who are unmarried and sexually immoral
Idolators	Those who worship false gods or follow a false religion
Adulterers	Married people who are sexually immoral (unfaithful to a spouse)
Effeminate	Those who allow themselves to be used unnaturally, including anyone who perverts the normal male-female roles as established by God
Abusers of themselves by mankind	Homosexuals, including anyone who perverts the normal male-female roles as established by God
Thieves	Those who plunder openly and by violence, based on greed
Covetous	Those who lust after what they don't have or what others have
Drunkards	Those who drink and fall under the influence of alcohol (Eph. 5:18)
Revilers	Those who destroy with their words
Extortioners	Those who take unfair advantage of others for their own financial gain, through embezzling, pyramid schemes, and the like

2. Scripture teaches that we will know whether someone is saved or not by his or her "fruit." A true Christian produces the fruit of the Spirit. What is in a person's heart will reveal itself in words and actions.
3. Washed, sanctified, justified.
4. *Washed*—When we accept Christ, our sins are washed away, and we are seen as clean. (The Greek word for "washed" means "to wash fully," "have remitted," "wash away." It is from another Greek word meaning "bathe completely off." *Sanctified*—An easy way to remember this meaning is to think of it as "saintified." We are set apart unto God from sin, a growing process that should see us acting more and more like saints. *Justified*—The righteousness of God has been imputed to us and, in His eyes, we are righteous. (The Greek word means to "render innocent," "to declare righteous." As Romans reiterates over and over, there is nothing we can do for justification. Justification is by faith in Christ's cleansing blood.)
5. Verse 1 shows positional sanctification ("we should be called the sons of God"). Verse 3 shows progressive sanctification ("every man that hath this hope in him purifieth himself"). Verse 2 shows perfect sanctification ("we know that, when he shall appear, we shall be like him").

6. The body is for the Lord, not for fornication or self-gratification.
7. Each believer is a "member of Christ" and part of His Body. When we commit fornication, it is like bringing Christ into the sin.
8. Joseph literally ran from the presence of Potiphar's wife, who was trying to entice him.
9. Personal answers. (Sexual intimacy affects our whole being, not just the physical. Especially for a woman, a strong emotional bond accompanies sex. When sexual sin occurs and the relationship breaks off, the emotional scars can be devastating. Sexual sin causes broken marriages, shattered homes, unwanted babies, heartache, and disease. It also may involve lying, cheating, bitterness, and a multitude of other sins.)
10. 1 Thess. 4:3–5—The will of God is for believers to stay away from fornication. Staying away from it is also part of sanctification and becoming more like Christ. We are to keep, or guard, our bodies in sanctification and honor. Prov. 5:3–12—Solomon warned his son to stay away from the "strange woman" and names possible consequences of giving in to lust: loss of honor, wealth, and health. Prov. 6:32–35—These verses talk about destroying one's own soul with adultery. An adulterer will have dishonor and reproach. Eph. 5:3—Speaking to the church at Ephesus, Paul says no one in the church should be known for fornication.
11. The precious blood of Christ.
12. To glorify God in his or her body and spirit.
13. Webster defines *glorify* as "to cause to be or treat as being more splendid, excellent, etc. than would normally be considered; to honor with praise, admiration or worship." Our bodies, as well as our spirits, should cause others to see God as splendid, excellent, and worthy of praise.

LESSON 6

1. Benevolence. It means "debt" in 1 Corinthians 7:3. (The husband and wife are to give to each other what is owed sexually. There should be mutual satisfaction.)
2. The principle is mutual submission. (Each spouse has power over the body of the other. When you marry, the needs of the other person come first. If your husband is asking for your body, he has every right to it. This will not become an area of selfishness when there is true *agape* [unconditional, self-sacrificing] love between husband and wife.)
3. "To deprive," "to keep back by fraud."
4. Mutual consent for fasting and prayer. (At times in the Old Testament, Israelite men were commanded to keep themselves from women in preparation for a meeting with God or a major event. You and your husband might decide to pray and fast [from food and sexual relations] before a big decision or an important event. Again, it is mutual and spiritual.)
5. So that Satan does not tempt you or your husband. (Protect your husband by not depriving him.)
6. Neither husband nor wife should divorce the other. If they do, they should remain unmarried or be reconciled.
7. Christ's teaching is that in marriage God makes man and woman one flesh

and that no one should ever divide it. He also states that if someone divorces and remarries, he or she has committed adultery.

8. A believer is married to an unbeliever, and the unbeliever decides to leave.
9. (a) The unbelieving spouse is "sanctified" by the believer, as are the children. (b) This is not in regard to salvation, or the spouse would not be called an unbeliever. The Greek word means "set apart." The presence of a believer causes the home to be set apart to God. All the blessings and graces that flow to that believer affect the home. The children will have a Christian influence if the couple stay together. That's why the believer is encouraged to stay, as in 1 Peter. The believer's influence and behavior may be what cause the unbelieving spouse to accept Christ.
10. A woman is bound by the law to her husband as long as he lives. She is not loosed unless her husband dies. If she marries another while her husband lives, she is an adulteress.
11. "Saving for the cause of fornication" and "except it be for fornication."
12. Joseph was "minded to put her away." (This is the term used for divorce throughout the Scriptures.)
13. (a) Husband. (b) No, they were not married yet.
14. Circumcision, employment, and marriage. (They were not to become circumcised just because they got saved, since "circumcision is nothing" when it comes to salvation. If they were servants, they were to remain as servants, ultimately serving Christ. Salvation also did not affect their marital status. If Paul thought marriage was preferable, he would have advised single Christians to marry, but either state is acceptable.)
15. The total focus of an unmarried person can be service to the Lord. A married person must consider his or her spouse and family.
16. Marriage is until death, but if a husband dies, a widow may remarry (but only in the Lord). Paul also states that in his opinion, she'd be happier staying single.

LESSON 7

1. (a) Knowledge and charity. (b) Knowledge puffs up, and charity edifies, or builds up.
2. That no one knows it all. (There is always more to learn.)
3. Loving.
4. Eating certain foods and observing certain feast days.
5. Verse 5—You should be fully persuaded in your mind about what you decide, having no doubts. Verse 6—Whatever you decide, you should do it as unto the Lord.
6. We are not to judge another's convictions. Every one of us will give account to God for what we did or did not do and for our motives.
7. Personal answers. (There is only one true God no matter what idols are called. The true God is God the Father and Jesus Christ, Who created all things.)
8. Neither—eating or not eating does not make us better or worse before God.
9. Make sure your liberty does not become a stumbling block to another believer.
10. Anything we put in the way of another believer, causing that believer to stumble in his or her Christian walk. (If you as a mature believer do

something that a newer Christian is convicted about, it may cause him to go against his conscience, and that would be sin, or it may be a source of grief to him.)

11. Sin. (When you cause a fellow believer to stumble, it is a sin against that believer and Christ. We often talk about our preferences being perfectly okay, but they can be a sin to us when we practice them without regard for our fellow Christians.)
12. Personal answers. (When Paul says that "all things are lawful," he is referring to activities not specifically forbidden in the Scriptures. All things may be permitted, but not all things are to our advantage or benefit us.)
13. Personal answers. (When a believer partakes in the Lord's Supper, he is partnering, or taking part, with Christ. We are in fellowship not only with other believers, but with Christ Himself.)
14. (a) No. (b) Partaking in an idol feast is the same as communing with devils. (Religious ceremonies, whether Christian or pagan, involve participation with other worshipers and the one being worshiped. So when it comes to pagan festivals, it is not just a matter of whether one should eat the meat offered to idols—a Christian should not be there at all.)
15. If it's sold in the marketplace, feel free to buy it, but don't ask questions about it. Idol meat is like any other meat in the marketplace. If you are invited to a banquet, eat what is placed in front of you unless someone brings to your attention that it was offered to idols, showing his concern. For his sake, don't eat it. That will protect your reputation and his conscience. (The second situation is not an idol feast as discussed in verses 14–22, but a feast in a home.)

LESSON 8

1. An apostle had to have seen the risen Christ. (Paul had seen Christ on the road to Damascus [Acts 9] and, therefore, referred to himself as the least of the apostles. An apostle also had to be commissioned by Christ, as Paul was on the road to Damascus.)
2. "My work in the Lord" and "the seal of mine apostleship." (In ancient times a seal was used on containers, letters, and other things to authenticate what was inside and to prevent alteration of the contents. The believers were Paul's "seal," showing the authenticity of his apostleship, the proof of his genuineness.)
3. To eat and drink, be married, and minister without having to work on the side.
4. A soldier, a farmer, and a shepherd. A soldier's expenses are taken care of while he (or she) is serving; one who plants a vineyard is sustained with the fruit; and one who raises a flock receives of the milk of the flock.
5. Those that minister in the temple live off the sacrifices of the temple. (They did not work outside the temple.)
6. They received of the heave offering whatever was not consumed in the fire. Every oblation (meat offering, sin offering, trespass offering) would partly be for the priests and their families. They received the best of the oil, the wine, and the wheat, as well as the firstfruits of everything grown in the land.
7. Those who minister the gospel should be able earn their living by the gospel.

8. Paul did not want to be a burden to the churches. He often looked after them like newborns, who certainly could not have cared for him.
9. He entered into business with Aquila and Priscilla as a tentmaker, a trade he already knew.
10. (a) That Paul was a chosen vessel to bear his name to the Gentiles, kings, and Israel. (b) That Paul's purpose was to be a minister and a witness to the Gentiles.
11. The Word of God became like a burning fire in his bones. He was exhausted from trying to fight it and had to speak God's Word.
12. *Dispensation* means "an administration, a stewardship." Paul had been entrusted with the gospel to "manage."
13. (a) Jews, those under the law. (b) Personal answers. (In his determination not to offend, Paul would keep the Mosaic law, though he was not obligated to do so. In that way, Jews could not find fault with him and might even listen to him reason ["argue," "discuss"] from the Scriptures that Jesus is the Christ.)
14. (a) "Those without the law," or the Gentiles. (b) Personal answers. (He did not try to keep the Mosaic law when giving the gospel to the Gentiles.)
15. He would not commit sin to be like the Gentiles. (Though Paul was not under the Mosaic law, he was under the law of Christ. He would not do anything that would go against the "law of Christ.")
16. The weak were those who had a strong conviction regarding a practice, possibly because they did not understand their freedom in Christ. (Paul would abstain from anything that might offend a weaker brother.)
17. Paul talks about being "temperate" in all things, fighting with a purpose (not as a boxer that swings at the air), and being self-disciplined. Paul brought his desires and his body under subjection so that he would not be disqualified from the race.
18. That believers should (1) lay aside every weight (anything holding us back, whether good or bad) and the sin that easily besets or thwarts us, and (2) run with patience, looking unto Jesus—the finish line!

LESSON 9

1. No. (Abraham became the father of all who believe. With Israel's unbelief, Gentile Christians are grafted in, replacing those branches, and share in the blessings promised to Abraham in the Abrahamic Covenant as his spiritual children [Rom. 11:11–24]. This does not mean, however, that the church has replaced Israel as the heirs of God's promises.)
2. Under the cloud—During daylight, God led the Israelites with a cloud, which became a pillar of fire by night. Passed through the sea—They were all delivered from the Egyptian army in the crossing of the Red Sea. (Every one of the Israelites experienced the miraculous guidance and deliverance of God.)
3. (a) Baptism is a believer's identification with Christ. (b) The Israelites were followers of Moses, recognizing him as their spiritual, God-appointed leader. (There was unity as they followed him.)
4. Manna and water were miraculously provided for Israel in the wilderness.

The meat and drink are called "spiritual" because they came directly from God. (The rock that the water came from symbolizes Christ, from Whom the Corinthian believers had eaten [the Bread of Life] and drunk [living water].)

5. (a) The report of the ten spies who lacked faith in Him. (b) They did not think they could claim the land promised to them by God. (c) Personal answers. (Hebrews 11:6 says, "Without faith it is impossible to please him.")
6. Answers may vary.

Sin	Occasion and Reference	Definition of This Sin
Lust	The Israelites lusted for the food they had had in Egypt (Num. 11:4–6).	Strong, inordinate desire (noun); to crave, covet, or set your heart upon (verb)
Idolatry	The incident with the golden calf (Exod. 32:1–14).	The worship of images or created objects (e.g., sun, moon)
Fornication	Israel committed whoredom ("prostitution") with the people of Moab (Num. 25:1–9).	Sexual immorality (noun); fornicate (verb): to act the harlot; to indulge in unlawful lust
Tempt Christ	The Israelites complained about having only manna to eat. This resulted in God sending serpents among them (Num. 21:4–6).	To test thoroughly; to try presumptuously; to provoke
Murmuring	When the spies returned with an evil report, the people began murmuring (Num. 14:35–37). The people murmured because of God's judgment on Korah. As a result they were consumed with a plague (Num. 16:41–49).	Grumbling; saying anything in a low tone; indignant complaining

7. For our example to admonish us not to commit the same sins.
8. (a) Personal answers. (Philippians 2:14 and 1 Peter 4:9 are possibilities.) (b) Joy and gratitude. (See, for example, Ephesians 5:20, Philippians 4:4, and 1 Thessalonians 5:16, 18.)
9. Personal answers. (Examples from the Old Testament were given not only to warn the Israelites but also to instruct and warn us not to commit these sins in these last days.)
10. Personal answers. (*Temptation* means "enticement" or "temptation to sin." It may include "testing" as with a trial, but with the result of trying our faith. There is still a temptation in any testing to not trust the Lord or to be bitter.)
11. (a) No. (Man is tempted, or enticed, and that can lead to sin. We know the temptation itself is not sin, because Christ was tempted [Matt. 4].) (b) The temptation comes, which can prey upon the lust of our flesh. When we give in to that lust, either enjoying it internally or acting upon it externally, it becomes sin. Sin leads to death.
12. (a) Lust of the flesh (anything that appeals to the flesh, e.g., sexual sins, gluttony); lust of the eyes (coveting, jealousy, etc.); and the pride of life (desire for power, popularity, etc.). (b) Personal answers.

13.

Reference	Lust of the Flesh	Lust of the Eyes	Pride of Life
Genesis 3:6	"Saw that it was good for food"	"Pleasant to the eyes"	"Desired to make one wise"
Matthew 4:1–10	"Command that these stones be made bread"	"Throw yourself down and the angels will bear thee up"	"All these things will I give thee"

14. God will not allow us to be tempted above what we are able. He will always make a way to escape so that we do not have to give in to temptation. This is not a promise to give us a way out of a difficult circumstance; it is a promise that we do not have to sin in any trial or give in to any temptation.

LESSON 10

1. God → Christ → man → woman.
2. Christ submitted Himself to God the Father as His head, but Christ was equal to the Father in every way.
3. Eph. 1:22–23—Christ is the head of the Body, the church. Eph. 5:22—The husband is the head of the wife.
4. Eph. 5:24—The church is subject to Christ and the wife to her husband. Eph. 6:1—Children are subject to their parents. Rom. 13:1—All are subject to government.
5. Having their heads covered.
6. Woman was created from the man and for the man.
7. Women naturally have longer hair, and they do not generally go bald.
8. Women and men are equal in the Lord and need each other. Roles are different in function but not in importance or spirituality.
9. There were divisions and factions among the believers, not unity. Further, there was greed instead of generosity. The wealthier ones would consume their food quickly rather than share it, and some were getting drunk.
10. The beginning of the exodus from Egypt, when the death angel "passed over" the Israelites and did not take their firstborn because the lamb's sacrificial blood was spread on their door lintels and side posts.
11. Jesus took the cup twice.
12. The bitter herbs would represent the bitter bondage they were in. The unleavened bread reminded them of their hasty flight from Egypt, where God told them to take unleavened bread. Reasons for unleavened bread: There was no time for the bread to rise, as they needed to leave immediately; leaven is used as a symbol of evil; and unleavened bread keeps better than bread with yeast. The lamb reminds them of the lamb sacrificed so that they would not die. His blood for theirs.
13. That cup followed the eating of the sacrificial lamb, also representative of the death on the cross of Jesus, the Lamb of God. The timing of the cross was also before the fourth cup, representing the coming of the kingdom.
14. We should never take the Lord's Supper "unworthily." We should examine ourselves before we partake.
15. Some examples would be having unconfessed sin, taking Communion as a

show to others, taking it without thought as to what it represents, or thinking about anything but the sacrifice of Christ's body and blood.

16. Some were weak (ill) and many slept (had died).

LESSON 11

1. Those that were speaking by the Spirit of God acknowledged Jesus as Lord.
2. Diversities of gifts (v. 4), of administrations (v. 5), and of operations (v. 6).
3. (a) All. (b) For the profit of all.
4.

Reference	Gift	Meaning
12:8	Wisdom	Skill in dispensing a clear understanding of doctrinal truths and wise application of the Scriptures
12:8	Knowledge	Ability to perceive and understand God's revelation (This gift was necessary for the writing of the Scriptures. Logically, it would precede the word of wisdom.)
12:9	Faith	An unusual ability to trust and rely on God (The person with this gift would be a great encouragement to those struggling with their faith.)
12:9	Healing	The ability to heal any affliction (The seventy sent out by Christ were given the gift of healing.)
12:10	Working of miracles	Any act contrary to natural design, explainable only by God's intervention (Casting out of demons would fall under this category.)
12:10	Prophecy	To speak forth or proclaim; it may mean "foretelling" or "forth-telling" (Miraculous foretelling was a temporary gift, but forth-telling is a continuous gift and is manifested today in the form of gifted preaching and even exhorting.)
12:10	Discerning of spirits	The supernatural ability of distinguishing true prophecies from false, Satanic ones
12:10	Tongues	Ability to speak in a language previously unknown to the speaker
12:10	Interpretation of tongues	Ability to interpret a language previously unknown to the interpreter

5. (a) No. The Holy Spirit distributes them "as He wills." (b) We don't have a part. Nowhere does Scripture tell us to seek a particular gift.
6.

Gift	Definition
Ministry serving	Serving
Teaching	Giving instruction, being a good communicator
Exhorting	To call near, implore, entreat
Giving	To share or impart
Ruling	To preside before
Showing mercy	Having compassion on

7. Brain—keeps the rest of the body working. Nerves—let us know when we are doing damage to a part of our body. Heart—pumps blood to every part to keep it alive. Eyes—give light to the entire body. Hands—carry out the purposes of the brain. Feet—allow us to balance and travel. Skeleton—gives us form and allows movement. (And those are only a few parts.)
8. (a) All believers. (b) Spirit baptism is the placement of the believer into the Body of Christ.
9. God does. (This verse taken with verse 11 equates the Holy Spirit with God—a support of the Trinity.)
10. (a) Paul compares the "lesser" gifts with the "uncomely" parts of the human body. (We may not be able to see our internal organs; they may not be lovely; but our bodies could not function without them.) (b) Personal answers. (A beautiful face, for example, may get noticed, but it is not as essential for a body to function.)
11. (a) Personal answers. (b) Personal answers.
12. When one member suffers, all the members suffer with it; and if one member is honored, all the members rejoice with him or her.
13. Apostles, who were eye-witnesses of Christ and appointed by Christ to serve Him; prophets, for the writing of Scripture; teachers, which probably refers to pastors.
14. Answers will vary. (This would be a good time to have each lady ask another woman in the class who knows her well what that woman think the lady's gifts are. See how the two answers compare with what the ladies wrote.)

LESSON 12

1. Tongues (v. 1); prophecy, wisdom ("understand all mysteries"), knowledge, faith (v. 2); and giving (v. 3).
2. (a) Possible answers: Giving can be all for show, vainglory, or recognition. (b) Personal answers. (One example is Ananias and Sapphira, who, trying to gain recognition for their gift, lied about the circumstances of their gift. They were both struck dead.)
3.

Verse	What Love Does	What That Means
13:4	Suffers long	Is patient, long-tempered
13:4	Is kind	Treats others with graciousness, with goodwill
13:4	Does not envy	Is not jealous
13:4	Doesn't vaunt itself; isn't puffed up	Does not brag; is not arrogant
13:5	Doesn't behave unseemly	Doesn't act inappropriately or unbecomingly
13:5	Seeks not her own	Is never selfish; serves
13:5	Is not easily provoked	Is not easily irritated or upset
13:5	Thinks no evil	Does not keep account of ("keep track of") wrongs
13:6	Rejoices in truth, not iniquity	Rejoice in the truth of God's Word, not in unrighteousness

Verse	What Love Does	What That Means
13:7	Bears all things	Covers; supports; protects from harm or ridicule
13:7	Believes all things	Gives confidence and trust
13:7	Hopes all things	Does not give up on things but keeps hoping
13:7	Endures all things	Holds fast

4. (a) The gifts were necessary because the baby church had only partial knowledge and revelation. (b) The Scriptures were not yet complete, so these sign gifts were necessary for authentication of the message.
5. God bore witness to the apostles' message through these gifts.
6. As we behold ourselves in the Word, we should become "doers" of that Word, then we will be blessed.
7. (a) Prophesying is better because it edifies, exhorts, and comforts. (b) If no one can interpret, tongues are spoken unto God, not to men. They edify no one but the speaker.
8. Personal answers. (If instruments produce an uncertain sound, no one has learned anything or knows how to respond. The same with tongues. If someone speaks with tongues without an interpreter, that person will be seen as a barbarian and will be speaking "into the air.")
9. If no one understands what is being said, the group cannot be edified; they cannot be blessed; they cannot say amen.
10. Tongues were to be a sign to the unbeliever, not the believer, whereas prophesying was for the believer to grow and be edified.
11. (a) The unbelievers would think the believers were crazy. (b) There would be conviction and changed lives as God's words were communicated.
12. To edify ("build up") and mature the believers.
13. Not more than two or three were to speak in tongues, and then only one at a time ("by course"). And someone should interpret. If there was no interpreter, then no one should speak aloud.
14. Prophets were to number no more than two or three. If a new revelation was given to a prophet, it would take precedence. They were also to prophesy one by one, not all at once.
15. Women were to keep silence; they were not to prophesy or speak in tongues.
16. All things were to be done in an orderly fashion, because God is not the author of confusion.

LESSON 13

1. Personal answers.
2. Personal answers. (The phrase refers to a miscarriage or premature birth. Paul may have been saying that his conversion could be compared to a premature birth and that he, unlike the mature and nurtured apostles, was thrust suddenly into apostleship without the nurture and teaching provided by Christ.)
3. Christ was not risen (v. 13). The apostles' preaching was vain, or empty, worthless (v. 14). The Corinthians' faith was also empty (v. 14). The apostles could be called false witnesses (v. 15). The Corinthians were still in their sin

(v. 17). Those who have died have perished permanently (v. 18). We are miserable (v. 19).

4. (a) The firstfruits were the beginning of the harvest. They provided a sample of what the rest of the harvest would be like. (As Romans 11:16 infers, whatever the firstfruits of a tree were like, they represented the rest of the tree. Firstfruits in the offerings to God symbolized the consecration of the entire harvest and were a pledge of what was to be gathered.) (b) Christ's resurrection is the promise of what is to come—the promise of future resurrections.
5. Those that have died in Christ will rise at the Rapture, before living believers are taken up.
6. (a) Christ will deliver up the kingdom to the Father. (b) This refers to the end of the Millennium when the last resurrection takes place. At that time, Creation will be restored and redeemed and given to the Father as Christ's last act of His subjection to the Father. In the eternal state, all things will be under the administration of the triune God.
7. "That they may obtain a better resurrection."
8. Eat and drink, for tomorrow we die.
9. The hope of seeing Christ and becoming like Him (the resurrection).
10. The seed and the body must both die before anything rises. A seed bursts open and becomes whatever type of body of grain was contained in the seed, put there by God. A body must die before it can be raised again, still a body, but in a different form. (Each person has the body given to him or her by God—though the resurrected body is different from the "seed," it is still the physical body. When Christ died and rose again, He rose with a physical body that could eat and drink, but it was different in that He could go through walls, appear instantly, and vanish from sight. His glorified body was the same, but different!)
11. (a) The body is sown in corruption but raised in incorruption (v. 42), sown in dishonor but raised in glory (v. 43), sown in weakness but raised in power (v. 43), sown a natural body but raised a spiritual body (v. 44). (b) Our resurrected bodies will never again be subject to deterioration or death; they will be perfected to never sin again, always honorable; they will be strong, never again weak or sick; and we will no longer be limited to the physical natural world. (Praise the Lord!)
12. The Lord will descend with a shout, the voice of the archangel, and the trump of God. The dead in Christ will be raised from their graves with glorified bodies, and those living will be instantly changed into their new bodies. Then we will all meet the Lord in the air.
13. Believers' bodies are changed.
14. Because we will rise again and have victory over death, we can be faithful and steadfast in service, knowing that this life is not the end.
15. (a) The first day of the week. (b) According to how God had prospered them.
16. Be alert, be firm in the faith, be mature, be strong, and be loving.
17. Stephanas, Fortunatus, and Achaicus.